Anti-Racism Education

Anti-Racism Education
Theory and Practice

George J. Sefa Dei

Fernwood Publishing
Halifax

Editing: Anne Webb
Design and production: Beverley Rach
Printed and bound in Canada by: Hignell Printing Limited

A publication of:
Fernwood Publishing
Box 9409, Station A
Halifax, Nova Scotia
B3K 5S3

Fernwood Publishing Company Limited gratefully acknowledges the financial support of The Ministry of Canadian Heritage and the Canada/Nova Scotia Cooperation Agreement on Cultural Development.

Canadian Cataloguing in Publication Data

Dei, George Jerry Sefa, 1954-
Anti-Racism Education

Includes bibliographical references.
ISBN 1-895686-63-6

1. Multicultural education -- Canada. 2. Racism -- Study and teaching -- Canada.
3. Canada -- Race relations -- Study and teaching.
I. Title. II. Series.

LC1099.5.C3D44 1996   370.19'342'0971   C95-950337-4

Contents

To my mother, Afua Donkor (alias Agnes Koduah)

Acknowledgements

I could not have written this book without the intellectual, moral and material support of many people from the conception of the project to its completion. Foremost, I would like to thank my family for their patience and understanding and for putting up with those hours that I was absent from the home working on the project. To my partner, Nana, thank you for being there for me and for offering the needed encouragement. My eight year old son, Prince, might have wondered about the long hours I spent outside the home last summer. I thank him for not complaining to dad. To my mother, Afua; my brother, Kwabena; and my two sisters, Afua and Auntie Amma, I sincerely appreciate the many ways you all inspired and comforted me. I am indeed blessed to have this family to count on.

Many years of anti-racism praxis precede this work and I acknowledge the work of all those who have taught me directly and indirectly. I have benefited immensely from my academic association and social contact with many students, faculty and staff of the Ontario Institute for Studies in Education, Toronto. These associations gave me the necessary knowledge to undertake this project. I cannot mention the names of all those who have been instrumental and influential in the development of my academic and political thoughts. To the students in my graduate level courses—1947: Principles of Anti-Racism Education; 1948: The Sociology of Race and Ethnicity; and 1979: Modernization, Development and Education in African Contexts—I owe a great deal of intellectual debt. In varied ways many of you challenged me to think, teach and act critically, and to always look for that vital connection between theory and practice in the "act" of education. The many students who worked with me on my various research projects, particularly Leilani Holmes, Josephine Mazzuca, Elizabeth McIsaac and Bethlehem Kidane, taught me about perseverance, dedication and giving time to others. Intellectually and politically, I have "grown" from the engagements with many other colleagues, notably Agnes Calliste, Budd Hall, Patience Elabor Idemudia, Sherene Razack, Anita Sheth, Rinaldo Walcott and Handel Kashope Wright.

I gratefully acknowledge the contributions of Jeffrey Kugler, Andrew Thornton, Doreen Fumia, Moon Joyce, Bobby Blanford, Andenye Chablitt-Clark, Marcia James and others who read earlier chapters or portions of this book.

Jeffrey and Andrew need special mention because they spent a great deal of their time critiquing and offering valuable suggestions that have improved this work. I have sometimes wondered whether Jeffrey saw this book as a "personal project." I will remain indebted to Andrew and Andenye for their assistance in responding to the editor's suggestions concerning issues of clarity and the elaboration of ideas.

Special gratitude also goes to Olga Williams for her word processing skills and for the time spent proofreading initial drafts of this book. And, finally, to the folks at Fernwood Publishing—Errol Sharpe, Beverley Rach, Brenda Conroy, Chauna James, Donna Davis and especially Anne Webb—I say a big thank you for publishing this book and for your constructive comments, insights and suggestions.

George J. Sefa Dei
Toronto, September 1995

Preface

Every day in North America, educators walk into classrooms which differ profoundly from those they attended when they were children. For some of these teachers, it is as if they experienced learning as children and young adults in a different universe from that experienced by the children they teach. No matter what a teacher's social location might be in terms of race, ethnicity, class and gender, that educator is most likely interacting on a daily basis with learners with backgrounds and experiences different from his or her own.

Every day in North America, students negotiate, in the course of interacting with one another, issues around race, class, gender and ethnicity. One child calls another a racial or sexist name, and a fight breaks out in a playground. Students surround and comment on a little girl whose hair looks "different." High school students meet to discuss a push for African Studies classes, or the integration of Black/African history courses into the curriculum. An opposing group says they feel excluded. A student who feels her religion is misunderstood by others talks about her religion in class.

School teachers, counsellors, administrators, janitors, cafeteria workers, bus drivers and other staff members address racial and ethnocultural difference in their schools daily. Some do so by attempting to "keep difference from being explosive." One way they do this is by attempting to ignore and erase the differences that students bring to the classroom. However, increasing numbers of educators and administrators are tending to more equitably address racial and ethnocultural differences which students bring to the schools. But is what is currently being done enough?

This book addresses the theory and practice of anti-racism education, which is a proactive, process-oriented approach to helping educators and students negotiate and gain insight into the racial and ethnocultural differences they may bring to the classroom. Anti-racism education has a rich theoretical base, and an everyday practical grounding for educators who wish to both understand and engage issues of racial and ethnocultural difference in their classrooms. It is also about investigating and changing how schools deal with issues of White privilege and power-sharing.

The increasing racial diversity in North American classrooms means that the everyday classroom interactions of students and instructors are not only richer in variety, but more complex. The increasing ethnocultural diversity in our schools means that the histories, cultures and everyday experiences students, teachers and administrators bring to the classroom are often quite distinct and separate, even distanced by time and space. Teachers, in particular, are faced with the task of helping one another, and their students, to engage positively, negotiate fairly, and intellectually come to understand "difference" in their classrooms.

The importance of this daily task cannot be stressed enough. The ways in which the next generation learns to engage, negotiate, struggle over and understand "differences" are crucial to the future of North America. The "social crises" (budgetary, political and medical) that North Americans face are indeed imperative concerns, yet we often ignore this real question: How can we value our differences and equitably share power? This may be the determining question as we move into the twenty-first century and beyond. Anti-racism theory and practice offer some ways in which we can confidently address this question in our classrooms, schools, playgrounds and neighbourhoods.

Many well-meaning Canadians are increasingly questioning educational practices (curriculum, texts, pedagogies) that do not speak adequately to the variety and richness of human experiences, or to the diverse history of events and intellectual ideas that have shaped human growth and development. Many Canadians see anti-racism education as one way to address the problems associated with the school being a site for reproducing societal inequalities. The theoretical and practical underpinnings of anti-racism education are being (re)formulated, specifically considering the context of Canadian schooling and education. There is the need to examine what exactly anti-racism education is, and how it can be incorporated into the various phases and aspects of the school system. For example, how can anti-racism education help in identifying the areas of systemic racism and power inequities within schools? How can anti-racism education assist in developing the student's sense of connectedness to, and identification with, the school? How can anti-racism education help in responding to broader questions of educational equity and social justice? How can Canadian schools develop and sustain a commitment to uphold the teachings of anti-racism education? Educators, students and administrators must be prepared to make an unequivocal commitment to societal transformation and then to make concrete change as required.

This book addresses these important aspects of anti-racism debates, focusing on the Canadian schooling and educational context. It considers the challenges posed by anti-racism education through a critical examination of both the theory and practice of what anti-racism education entails, the strategies for its implementation and the implications for the various stakeholders in the Canadian education system. I use "critical" to imply a critique aimed at understanding and transforming existing ways of thinking and knowing and doing things. In this sense then critical theory is a social practice. I would also add that critique is not available only to "academics" but actually arises from many sites. Anti-racism

Preface

education is more than a theoretical discourse or abstract set of propositions; it is an approach which includes a commitment to political and academic education for meaningful social change.

This book is divided into seven chapters. Chapter One introduces discussion on the theory and practice of anti-racism education. Chapter Two examines basic principles of anti-racism education. Chapter Three scrutinizes the concept of race and the paradox of racism in the anti-racism discourse. It specifically examines theoretical approaches to the concept of race, focusing on anthropological and sociological analyses. Particular areas of discussion are the historical dimensions of race discourse in the Social Darwinist, early American, structuralist and functionalist schools of thought. The chapter also explores current ideological, stratification and socio-psychological approaches to race and racism. In making these distinctions, I am indebted to an outline for a course on The Paradox of Racism developed in the 1980s by Professor Frances Henry of York University.

While the centrality of race in the anti-racism debate is acknowledged, Chapter Four explores the relational aspects of social difference (race, class, gender, sexuality) in what is termed "integrative anti-racism." This chapter argues that a working knowledge of the intersections of race, class, gender and sexual oppression is helpful in fully addressing educational equity, social justice and change.

Chapter Five looks at one model of anti-racism education. It examines the connections and contradictions between anti-racism and Afrocentric education. The chapter shows how Afrocentric knowledge is constructed and validated. Relevant connections are made to African cultural patterns and cultural production, while the legitimacy of Afrocentric perspectives in Euro-Canadian/American schooling is emphasized. The chapter also addresses the implications of Afrocentric knowledge for contemporary schooling and the education of students, in particular but not exclusively, of African descent in North America.

Chapter Six continues the discussion of education centred in students' cultural histories and ancestries by exploring the idea of Black-focused/African-centred schools in contemporary Canadian contexts. The position that these schools are separatist or segregationist is interrogated.[1] The chapter advances the argument that pitting the idea of "inclusive schooling" against a "focused education" is a false choice. Although the discussion is grounded in ongoing debates in the Province of Ontario, the chapter proceeds to examine the challenges posed for all Canadian students, parents, educators and administrators. Chapter Seven synthesizes the issues raised in the book, pointing to what the notion of an inclusive, integrative anti-racism education implies for future educational practice in Euro-Canadian/American contexts.

To conclude, I would like to point out that all education involves social and political power relations. Anti-racism education is no exception. However, I believe that unless anti-racism education is integrated with family life, home-care, daycare, schools and the various communities in which we live and work, all that can be hoped for is a fragmented, top-down approach to social change. Where the sites of anti-racism education are and at what age it "starts" are important factors to consider if this type of education is to be truly transformative. I have positioned my discussion to focus on Canadian schooling contexts, but I invite readers to view the discussion from the social location in which they are positioned. I want every reader to see how we (both the reader and I) are implicated in the discussion, particularly our ways of seeing or doing things in diverse social settings.

Note

1. The term "interrogated" is used to demonstrate a personal/political struggle and radical engagement with issues of race, racism and anti-racism. This metaphor is most useful because it suggests a more explicitly political engagement on the part of the reader than terms like "examined," for example. The concept of "examine" leaves the reader in the position of not being directly involved in the process. Race, racism and anti-racism education become somehow containable within a glass box and we then extract bits and pieces of them to "examine" under the lens of our anti-racism "microscope." This metaphorical distancing from racism is one part of the problem of racism. A partial remedy is the use of the term interrogate.

Chapter One
Introduction

Practice and experience should be the contextual basis of social and intellectual knowledge. Educators should not conveniently separate the everyday practices they are involved in from academic formulations and conceptualizations about our social world. Everyone is differentially burdened by the history of racism[1] and all other discriminations in society. Despite what some have rightly called a "crisis of knowledge" in post-modern[2] society, I believe most radical and progressive educators can (re)appropriate existing "common-sense" understandings of how racism and other forms of oppression function to serve and deny certain interests in society. Educators have a duty to use such knowledge and understanding, not only to assist in the project of academic theorizing about our everyday world, but also to engage in a visionary political project for social transformation.

I set out to write this book from my vantage point as a male, African-Canadian educator. In telling the story of how I see anti-racism unfolding in Euro-Canadian/American contexts, I have chosen to fall back on my African cultural ancestry, historical background and lived experience(s). I acknowledge that there must be space in the story for other (African and non-African) experiences to be read and shared. I also acknowledge the important connections between African ways of knowing and other indigenous peoples' social knowledges that are grounded in historical material experiences. I do not use "other" in the colonial sense of "othering" (Said 1979), that being a process of objectification and construction of "other-ness" (see also Gupta and Ferguson 1992: 13). I am not interested in reading and interpreting the "other/self" dichotomy through the image of the "self/other" (even as "I" occupy the position of "other" to the hegemonic colonial/imperial White western "self"). I am using "other" in a progressive sense of political and cultural affirmation of difference. Such difference entails varied and alternative approaches to understanding our social, political and material world.

In broaching the subject of the social construction of anti-racism knowledge I will begin with myself as a positioned subject. Jameson, Eagleton and Said (1990), among many others, have stressed the importance of understanding the production and reproduction of knowledge and social meanings from diverse and variant vantage points (see also Tierney 1993a). Anti-racism educators, activists and students engage, and negotiate[3] on, social issues with a set of ideological and political assumptions about the nature and functioning of society. These assumptions also help us interpret society. Our knowledge, like all knowledge, is positional and reflects human interests. Our personal journeys reflect how we see the world (Banks 1995) and how, as individuals, we structure and engage in pedagogical and communicative practices (Sleeter 1995). Similarly, our individual political assumptions impinge upon how we each structure our pedagogical ideas about alternative educational visions. This is the context for the "personal and the political."

When I began the process of writing this book, I could not help but recall some educational experiences that have informed and influenced my thoughts about the need for and relevance of anti-racism education in Euro-Canadian/American contexts. I recalled the colonial education I received growing up in my birthplace, Ghana. My frustrations were not so much about what the colonial curriculum taught me, but even to this day I am angry about what was *not* taught. I have wondered in my later years why learning about Niagara Falls in Canada was more important than being taught about the local rivers in my village. After all, these were rivers in which I swam, bathed, caught fish and fetched water for household use. I also recalled my postgraduate education in anthropology and the many times I had to read anthropological accounts of African and non-Western peoples that were written in Eurocentric frames of reference. Some of my well-intentioned and critical teachers struggled unsuccessfully to critique and move away from such frames of reference.

Today, I acknowledge both my position of privilege, teaching in a Canadian institution of higher learning and, I must add, the contradictions that come with this position. I see so few people teaching in the academy who look and sound like me. I also continue to struggle with the fact that I am part of the "other" that has been misrepresented and portrayed as exotic for far too long in Euro-Canadian/American academic discourses and texts. I share with many "others" the common historical experience of the subjugation of our existence through the devaluing and deprivileging of our histories and ancestral knowledges within Euro-Canadian/American academic scholarship and thought. I also have to struggle with the fact that, in discussing issues of inclusivity and representation of the "other," I have to employ the language of those who historically and currently hold positions of power over me and my communities in society. However, I find it gratifying that I may have some practical experiences as "other" and of resisting racism which enhance my engagement in a critical dialogue about what "anti-racism" might mean.

As a minority faculty member working in the area of anti-racism education, it does not take long to hit a crossroad when engaging in the politics of anti-racism organizational change within mainstream, hetero-patriarchal academic institutions. This crossroad is a place where the "subject matter" of anti-racism education, my experiences and what they imply, and the concerns of my students, intersect. Increasingly, many students, particularly minority students, are challenging educators to be more inclusive in their pedagogies and other academic practices. I am hearing from students critical and oppositional discourses that challenge the culture of dominance of mainstream, hetero-patriarchal educational institutions in North America. The message I keep hearing from these students is that something is not right and needs changing. For example, in my graduate classes students continually ask why there are so few minority faculty in our institutions of higher learning and what it is going to take to "colour the Institute."

The crossroad is a place where I can bring these concerns and paths together, and begin to advance the notion of anti-racism education as a vehicle for social change.

In presenting these ideas and concerns, I ask the reader's permission *not to speak to*, but rather *to speak with* you. I do not intend to preach to anyone. In fact, I will ask the reader to resist being preached to. We live in a contemporary new epoch, one which is remarkably different in its celebration and acknowledgement of cultural fragmentation and pluralism. As a people seeking collectively to deal positively with difference and diversity in our schools, we must all be able to reflect and learn from the past and present, and to project into the future. Every educator should speak out boldly on the pertinent educational issues of our time, and also be able to articulate a clear and purposeful vision for educating both young and old for the future. There is a long history of individuals and communities speaking out to challenge our school systems to live up to the ideals of equipping all students with the necessary skills to function in and build multi-racial and multi-ethnic societies. Many youths have spoken about a sense of alienation and of the pain they experience because of their lack of connectedness to, and identification with, certain societal institutions. Despite the profound alienation and violation of many marginalized youths' histories and identities, they have successfully accomplished many important and positive things. History teaches us valuable lessons about the importance of understanding the diverse social realities and the contributions of all peoples. There are many lessons in history. History must teach us. If it does not, then it is not history worth talking about. We must not only reclaim marginalized histories, but also do new readings of dominant histories to restore and rewrite what was once excluded. This process will be arduous and painful, but politically and intellectually insurgent.

In interrogating the ongoing struggle of the Euro-Canadian/American school system to address the needs of a diverse student body, it is all too easy to take the dominant liberalized position that "we must give history a chance to correct itself." It is conveniently argued by some that inclusive education will happen as a matter of fact, given the changing dynamics of post-modern society.

This view ties in well with a popular refrain: "It is only a matter of time for the change to happen." I believe that we have to get rid of the idea that time can solve all social problems. All time does is pass by. As educators, administrators, students and parents, we have to act now and act steadfastly to address our pressing social and educational issues.

In many ways, social change is a form of political imagination. Change means we must find new ways of imagining ourselves as moral, political and social beings. We cannot afford to encourage any political ambivalence about the need to deal positively with diversity and difference. We need to search hard for positive alternative arrangements which meet the challenges of social diversity and educational inclusivity. We must act collectively and in a manner that is guided by our vision of a common good for all. A common good can only be determined in the actual practices and experiences of our diverse and differing communities. This search for a common good is an integral part of anti-racism politics and education.

In deciding how we can act collectively, perhaps we could learn from some African words of wisdom. There is an African proverb that says, "Rain does not fall on one roof and neither does the sun shine on one house alone." It is also said that, "One tree does not make a forest." There is another saying that, "One ant cannot build an anthill." And lastly, there is the fable that, "I am because we are, and because we are, therefore I am." One may ask: "What is the social/ educational message contained in these proverbs?"

These proverbs point to the importance of understanding the human condition and our connections with one another. They suggest that, as a society, we are bound together by a cloth of mutuality and respect for one another. No one is an island unto herself or himself. It is only through the love of sharing and protecting each other that as a society we can sustain the longevity of this cloth. Thus we all need to work together to develop our spiritual, emotional and collective well-being in order to understand, appreciate and realize our individual and collective destinies. We learn from each of the African fables that each of us, as a member of society, can never reach our full potential as long as others among us are not allowed to reach their goals and dreams. While the individual is extremely important, the notion of "individuality" only makes sense in relation to the larger community of which the individual is a part. Therefore, we must all rise above our individual concerns and strive for the common good of all.

These fables also caution against an "uncritical adulation of difference" (Amin 1994: 17) that centres the individual without an attempt to link the individual to the collective project. There is a risk of falling into the trap of rational, capitalistic, neo-conservative modes of thought that unproblematically extol our individual virtues. This can be seen in discourses concerning individual achievement, the power of meritocracy and the acceptance of individual responsibility. These neo-conservative reasonings lack critical interrogation of, and deny the role of, structural and systemic barriers to self- and group-actualization and development.

When insisting that human and social differences be recognized, it is important to connect the understanding of our individualities to the larger collective to which we all belong. To this end, an important question becomes: "For which reasons and to what ends do we recognize individual differences?" Difference is recognized as a source of strength to bolster our collective might. We act together to transform our social and material existence.

However, for the idea of "collective" to make any sense at all, there must be a strong belief in the idea that everyone of us has rights, duties and responsibilities. We have the right to demand a space in our community and to insist that all voices be heard. People can choose to be silent but they have a right to be heard. But we also have responsibilities that go with such rights. Those responsibilities have to be fulfilled if we are ever to satisfy both our individual and collective dreams and aspirations.

For example, in the task of educating the youth, students have responsibilities as members of the school body to educate themselves and to acquire the skills necessary to function in society. One responsibility of educators is to ensure that all students develop a shared sense of belonging, a sense of connection and a sense of identification with the school. Every youth in school has the right to be exposed to the diverse experiences, accounts and histories that have shaped, and continue to shape, human growth and development. Every student must be able to claim ownership of her or his school and be able to say: "This is my school, I see myself here, and I belong here."

Educators have a responsibility to deliver *the right of education* to youth. They have the responsibility to teach youth about the diversity of human experiences and to provide them with all the necessary skills required to function in contemporary society. Educators have the responsibility to bring to their students' attention social injustice and how everyone is implicated in the fight for justice and human dignity. Educators have the duty to let all students be aware of the racial, class, gender and sexual implications of whatever is taught in the classroom. They have a duty to teach about the scourge of racism, sexism, classism and other forms of social oppression. Educators have a responsibility to teach students about social and civic responsibility.

But, above all else, we, as a society, have collective responsibilities. We must never shy away from challenging our appointed leaders to live up to the ideals of a just society. We must ask that society listen and respond to the unheard voices, especially those of the youth, those less powerful in society and those emerging from "under the sink." These are the voices calling for power-sharing in society. This is not a call to have power over others, that is, to have power to control and dominate others. It is a call to have power to enrich oneself and allow each of us to take advantage of available opportunities in society. It is in such a vision of non-competitive, human co-existence that I locate the push for anti-racism studies and organizational change in society. To reach this understanding we must all come to appreciate the intersections of our racial, class, gender and sexual identities.

The current era of global economic restructuring, the "transnationalization of capital flows," "massive population movements," and a sophisticated global communication and information network have created new conflicts and contests among peoples, nation states and governments.[4] Without a doubt, these changes have also created new cultural and political spaces for the forging of alternative human and social interactions to deal with common human problems. These developments bear serious implications for radical educational politics of anti-racism change. We have to find new, workable ways to deal with the emerging globalization of racism. By this I mean ways to connect the issues creating human poverty, environmental abuse and the denial of human and collective rights through the process of the most powerful in our communities "designing futures" for others.

Despite some good intentions, society has so far not been successful in eradicating the menace of racism and other forms of oppression and discrimination. One of the challenges of anti-racism practice in the post-modern era is to call upon all critical and progressive educators and community workers to begin to forge new solidarities. These solidarities must recognize the tensions, conflicts and contradictions inherent to working across social and power differences. At the same time, such a realization should not immobilize progressive educators, workers and students and prevent them from acting to develop a common/shared vision of social transformation. New solidarities must seek to rupture the political, economic and ideological status quo and challenge society to side with the forces for social justice, peace and human dignity. The personal risks taken in advocating for social change are real and insidious, particularly given the mounting organized resistance against progressive change. These risks should be acknowledged. But the strength in our alliances will come from the development of a shared commitment to work for meaningful change. Sometimes alliances will be temporary and contingent, but we cannot have contingent moral commitments. We also need to reclaim "morality" from discourses of religiosity, fascists and the state. We need new discussions of public moralities and a moral public to inform our politics.

All progressive forces need to be included in the production, validation and dissemination of a critical anti-racism knowledge of social change. The inclusion of multiple voices from multiple social locations is one powerful way to rupture the institutional structures of society and to address questions of social credibility, fairness, justice and equity. Anti-racism educational knowledge, if articulated to focus on strategies for dealing with change, resistance and social transformation, can help students, educators and community workers develop a critical consciousness through a political agenda (see hooks 1988: 32; Hall 1993; and Novac 1994: 64).

Conceptual and analytical frameworks for understanding and interpreting society must be grounded in individual and collective lived experiences. There also has to be a grounded understanding of how, as individuals and groups, we are differently and differentially implicated in ways of knowing and articulating social experiences. There is no need to mystify or reify social reality in order to understand individual and collective lived experiences. However, in order to understand and appreciate each other and our society we must listen to and hear each other.

We live in a world where many still have lingering doubts about the social justification for addressing the social ills of racism and other forms of human oppression. Many do not have the courage or the space and voice to say exactly what we do not like about society. Compounding this problem is the fact that the post-modern society has to deal with complex, contradictory and often times complicated interpretations of the language of race and racism (see Kailin 1994: 180).

This book moves beyond the more abstract academic debates about the theoretical significance of race. I engage in a more grounded discussion on the social meaning of race and its intersections with other forms of social difference and oppression. I see an urgent need for a pre-eminent inclusiveness in the production, interrogation and dissemination of critical knowledge of race, social difference and oppression.

Anyone who seeks to interrogate and understand social relations is confronted with certain fundamental questions about their own histories and identities. For example, how do we theorize on the factors accounting for invidious distinctions between groups socially and politically defined as races (Banton 1979; White and Frideres 1977). Are there significant differences among groups within the human species? What are they and how can they be explained (Banton 1967)? How do we articulate, negotiate and relate to our human differences? How do the processes of "racial formation" (Omi and Winant 1994) account for our understanding of racial classification and oppression?[5] What are the ways through which race and anti-racism knowledge are being created, produced and disseminated in society? How does the current social formation provide the structures within which values, ideas and norms of dominant groups are hegemonized in society? How do relations of production affect the production and understanding of race knowledge? How do racial ideology and other ideologies help to stabilize social relations in the service of modern capital (Holmes 1994: 11)? How are racial politics played out in the structures and practices of society? How is racial domination sustained in society? How do the power relations in society influence the structure and dynamics of social difference?

I examine these questions in this book by engaging an anti-racism critique of the processes of schooling and education in the Canadian context. Throughout this book I conceptualize "schooling" as those formal structures, institutions and practices which take place within the jurisdictional and political boundaries of actual schools, universities, religious and state institutions (the military, for example). "Education" is used much more broadly to refer to all forms of learning and teaching, but also includes the educational experience of formal schooling institutions. My conception of education refers to activities which take place beyond the confines of those social structures, yet form a large part of the identity and knowledge of all students. This conception includes consuming popular music, playing on sports teams, watching television and movies as forms of and sites for educational experiences (Giroux 1981; hooks 1994). Within Canadian schools, educators are still working to identify how the issues of race identity and representation implicate or have a bearing on learning outcomes for youths. Many poignant questions are being asked by educators, students, parents, guardians, care-givers and community workers about the Euro-Canadian/ American education system. Their questions import that educational research must examine not only how schools promote academic success, but also how schools are engendering student failures. This means that educational research should critically interrogate the role of schools in the education process.

Educational researchers do not have to assume the position of those schools and school authorities that systematically shift blame onto students by pathologizing families and home cultures. The idea of passing on the responsibility of education to others in society must be questioned. When it is said that education is a shared responsibility among various stakeholders (students, teachers, administrators, parents and local communities), it means that no one can conveniently deny responsibility. For example, as schools deservedly take some credit for students' successes, they must not, at the same time, shy away from accepting partial responsibility for the failures. The same goes for parents and all other stakeholders in the education system. We must expect students to own up to their individual and social responsibilities. But we cannot, and should not, hold youths individually responsible for every social problem they encounter in their lives.

It has been rightly argued that structural processes of schooling and education provide unequal opportunities, and create differential outcomes for students, according to race, ethnicity, gender, sexuality, religion, culture, class and disability (see McCarthy and Crichlow 1993). A critical examination of the complex interactions of race, ethnicity, class and gender within our educational institutions provides some insight into how schools function to engage some students, while disengaging others. School administrators and educators, in particular, need to comprehend fully why schools fail some youths and, conversely, why some students are failing school.

As May (1994) points out, in trying to understand the issues of educational experiences of students, liberal-democratic theories of education tend to focus on family-school relations, conceptualizing schools and homes as sites and sources of student educational problems and pathologies. Reproduction theories of schooling, on the other hand, focus on how the structural processes of schooling create unequal outcomes, particularly for racial minority students and those from poor socio-economic family backgrounds. However, what is never adequately examined by such theories is how the structural processes of schooling are mediated by oppositional cultures and individual and collective forms of student resistance (see Willis 1977, 1983; Giroux 1983a, b; Apple 1986; McCarthy 1990; Ellsworth, 1992).

Conflict theorists, when examining the school's role in the unequal distribution of rewards, resources and opportunities in society, accord primacy to the dictates of capital (see Bowles and Gintis 1976). They fail to explore how the labour demands of the economy shape schools and the processes of schooling, and vice versa. Critical/radical educational theorists (Giroux 1983a; Apple 1986; McCarthy 1990) have drawn attention to how schools function to reproduce the dominant ideologies of society. Their examination of differential power relations within society, and how these affect the processes of delivering education, has provided us with an understanding of how the ideology of public schooling works to maintain the status quo. But schools are not only agencies for cultural, political and economic reproduction, they are also sites of contestation between groups differentially situated in terms of power relations. Critical ethnographies of schools reveal instances of resistance in which both students and educators are challenging the prevailing culture of dominance (see, for example, the works of Solomon 1992; Ibrahim 1994; Dei, Holmes, Mazzuca, McIsaac and Campbell 1995).

A contemporary educational and pedagogic challenge is to understand the nature of racial and ethnic minority student/educators' resistance to the power of schools to dominate subordinate groups, through definitions of *what is acceptable* and *what is not acceptable*; what is *valid knowledge* and what is *not valid knowledge*. Within Euro-Canadian/American schools there is a constant "ordering of knowledge" (Giroux 1984) through the process of giving recognition and validation to the experience and knowledge of some groups, while denying that of others (Castenell and Pinar 1993). Through the school's curriculum, educators and students are provided with academic definitions of what counts as valid knowledge and how such knowledge should be produced and disseminated. For marginal voices, the school curriculum and pedagogic practices have become sites for contesting their marginality and expressing opposition to the traditional roles of schools. By "curriculum" I mean the written and stipulated rules, codes of conduct, norms and values of the school, as well as the manner in which issues are taken up in academic texts and classroom discussions (see Apple and Taxel 1982). I am also referring to the "unwritten practices and procedures that influence student activities, behaviours, perceptions and outcomes" (Mukherjee and Thomas n.d.: 7), and serve to give schools their character (Bhyat 1993: 12).

Conceptualizing the school as a site for both student conformity and resistance allows educators to understand how alternative knowledges and pedagogies can be developed from everyday school practices and interactions.

Current calls for "alternative pedagogies," "inclusive curriculum" and "representative school environments" must be understood as challenges to the hegemonic Euro-centred norms, values and ideas that characterize Canadian schools. Educators and school administrators have to lead the way by opening up spaces in which alternative, non-hegemonic viewpoints can flourish in the schools. Educators must interrogate (rather than cursorily dismiss) alternative ideas and viewpoints on schooling—particularly those emanating from subordinated groups in society—and identify sources of students' cultural, political and intellectual empowerment and disempowerment. The interrogation, validation and incorporation of, for example, African-centred ways of knowing should not be seen as a move to replace one hegemonic form of knowledge with another or to denigrate Euro-Canadian/American scholarship in a bid to foster an oppositional discourse. Rather, it must be viewed as a call for Euro-Canadian/American schools to be more inclusive and to inform students about the diversity of human experiences. Schools should develop learning environments that are inclusive and caring, and foster respect, encouragement and self-worth among *all* students. An inclusive school environment must inspire a commitment to learning and ground such learning in the cultural heritage and ancestry of historically marginalized students and in their relation to dominant oppressive histories.

In an analysis of schooling and educational practices in Euro-Canadian/American contexts, it is important that we understand how the social and ideological processes of a racialized society are produced and reproduced in the everyday practices of schools. The school environment must become an open place of ideas where both official forms of knowledge and cultural, personal and oppositional forms of knowledge can be interrogated and allowed to flourish without boundary restrictions (i.e., restrictions in the form of conventional processes of legitimation and validation) (see Banks 1993).[6]

The issues of race and racism are particularly central to the schooling and educational experiences of minority students. In the search for an understanding of how and why schooling and education processes tend to engage some students while disengaging others, culture and race should not be seen as one category. Both analytical concepts are social constructs with immediate and profound significance in the daily lives of all students. To understand the mediation of culture and race and the dynamics of social difference in schooling, a discursive framework of anti-racism education needs to be engaged.

The recent emphasis on addressing the problematic issues concerning culture and cultural differences in the schools is not misplaced. However, it is important that, as educators address the current and future challenges of diversity and difference in school populations, the task of mobilizing to address cultural issues be expanded to include race issues as well. This calls for a new theoretical/discursive framework for understanding the sociology of race and schooling that emphasizes the roles of power and social conflict as the crucial variables in intergroup relations. It also means we must interrogate the processes by which certain groups are singled out for unequal treatment on the basis of real or imagined phenotypical characteristics.

Current thinking on race and anti-racism education must be expanded to include a critical interrogation of the economic, political, social and ideological processes and structures of society for their role in sustaining contemporary forms of what may be termed "anti-different" racisms.[7] The reality of contemporary society is that ideological and cultural practices of dominant groups do have a variety of material consequences for subordinated groups (Troyna 1993; Kailin 1994). Therefore, we need to understand how race knowledge is organized, structured, produced and received, and the implications for the material well-being of those who have historically occupied the margins of Canadian society (given their racial, ethnic, gender and class backgrounds). We need to ask questions about the particular ways of knowing about ourselves, and how we, as individuals and groups, construct and understand social differences and our multiple subjectivities. Such an understanding can become the cornerstone for a progressive politics of anti-racism organizational change.

Notes

1. See for example Kobena Mercer, "Black Art and The Burden of Representation." *Third Text* 10 (Spring 1990): 61–78, as an example of the differential burden of marginalized groups when engaging in cultural representation and transformation.

2. Throughout the text, I use "post-modern" to refer to an age of paradigmatic shift in knowledge, rejecting an essentialized reality or a universal, simplified definition of social phenomena. Post-modernism focuses on the complexities of lived experiences; it rejects the search for broad generalizations for local, specific/particularized and historically informed analysis grounded in spatial and cultural contexts (see also Parpart 1995). In the post-modern era there is a recognition of the "partiality and limits of knowledge," the celebration of difference(s) and the importance of recovering and hearing previously silenced voices. As many others have pointed out, the challenge is to determine how to situate the larger political-economic questions in the historically specific discussions of a post-modern era (see also Suleri 1992; Bhabha 1990).

3. In using the term "negotiate," I am trying to gesture towards a pedagogical stance which acknowledges power differentials among people who are engaged in pedagogical and political actions. Negotiate in this sense infers exactly the philosophy of an anti-racism praxis. It locates each of us in our pedagogical and political projects as having an interest in what happens, but also acknowledges that we are differently and differentially able to assert our power. In terms of knowledge production, it also means that "knowledge" is a negotiable or more open space than dominant Western Euro-Canadian/American traditions have held. Knowledge is itself a site of struggle and not a given quantity. This notion of negotiation then disrupts dominant traditions and demands that the voices of marginalized groups be heard from the outset.

4. See the introductory comments to the preliminary conference program of the Canadian Council of Area Studies Learned Societies (CCASLS), Ottawa, November 1994.

5. Here, I am extending Omi and Winant's (1994) use of the term "radical formation" to the historical processes through which individuals and groups became classified (and came to know themselves) as different races and subjected to differential and unequal treatment on the "basis of real or imagined characteristics" (Li 1990: 7). The process of racial formation is argued to be "a fundamental organizing principle of social relationships" (Omi and Winant 1994: 66) in Euro-Canadian/American societies. The understanding of these processes of racial formation are based on the notion of "race as an unstable and de-centred complex of social meanings constantly being transformed by political struggle" (ibid.: 68).

6. In an open academic setting, educators must expect to hear "oppressive" ideas and be prepared to deal with them. This means that classrooms become (in an obvious way) the site of very real political and intellectual struggle. This approach means that students and educators cannot retreat to the liberal humanist safety of simply "stating my opinion." An anti-racism pedagogy holds people accountable for what they say and do. It also recognizes that if people grow up in a racist world of misrepresentation and misinformation, then they cannot avoid having such beliefs and ideas as part of their knowledge base. A beginning point of anti-racism pedagogy is to take apart racist myths and misrepresentations.

7. By "anti-different" racisms, I mean the myriad forms of racisms based, not solely on perceived phenotypical differences between peoples, but also on a conflation of religious, cultural, class, language, gender and sexual differences among people (see also Macchiusi 1993: 60).

Chapter Two
Basic Principles
of Anti-Racism Education

The anti-racism discourse began in Britain before emerging in Canada, Australia and the United States. Among the early scholarly works that influenced and shaped the development of the anti-racism dialogue one can cite Mullard (1980, 1985), Brandt (1986), Troyna (1987), Troyna and Williams (1986), Gilroy (1982), Cohen (1988/9), Bains and Cohen (1988), Jeffcoate (1984), Nixon (1984), and Carby (1982) (see also Reed 1993, 1994). In Canada, the pioneering works of Abella (1984), Thomas (1984) and Lee (1985) served to lay the groundwork for anti-racism education as a serious academic and political project. The first of their objectives was to transform schooling and education. The impetus for anti-racism change came from local community political struggles which challenged the Canadian state to live up to the true meanings of democratic citizenship, social justice, equity and fairness.

Anti-racism education may be defined as an action-oriented strategy for institutional, systemic change to address racism and the interlocking systems of social oppression. Anti-racism is a critical discourse of race and racism in society and of the continuing racializing of social groups for differential and unequal treatment. Anti-racism explicitly names the issues of race and social difference as issues of power and equity rather than as matters of cultural and ethnic variety. A critical anti-racism discursive framework seeks a broad definition of race and racism that extends beyond the view that skin colour is the only signifier of difference. The historical processes of European colonization, cultural and political imperialism, and enslavement of the world's indigenous and non-White peoples are juxtaposed to simplistic notions of racial domination and difference based on skin colour and "natural" difference. This juxtaposition is designed to lead to a discussion and understanding of how current processes of racialization manifest themselves in post-modern society (see Miles 1989; Abdo 1993; Khayatt 1994; Reed 1994). Through the process of racializing society, social groups are distinguished and subjected to differential and unequal treatment on the basis of supposedly biological, phenotypical and cultural characteristics (Miles 1982; Li 1990: 7; Bolaria and Li 1988; Banton 1979). The new social markers of difference are being made and re-made in discourses around language, politics, culture and religion.

As an approach to educational transformation, anti-racism has social and political relevance and meaning to students, teachers and administrative staff, as well as to parents and local communities. Contemporary society is differentiated along many social lines; consequently, individuals and social groups are implicated differently in the politics of social change. Anti-racism discourse argues that educators, students and community workers cannot claim to remain neutral in the provision and utilization of educational knowledge. The claim to "neutrality" is itself a value-laden position (see Spivak 1993 on "Essentialism"). The political and academic practices of educators, administrators, students, parents and community workers shape, and are themselves shaped by, the daily lived experiences of society. How we interpret our social world (and subsequently attempt to transform it) is a consequence of such experiences. The processes of creating and legitimizing knowledge about society cannot, and should not, be discussed in isolation from the context, goals and purpose of education. Anti-racism education is not the advancement of knowledge for its own sake. Rather, the purpose of anti-racism education is to help create a just and humane society for the well-being of all people.

There are moral and immoral aspects of education. Anti-racism education does not pretend otherwise. Its social and educational agenda is to rupture the status quo through the social and personal commitment to political activism of the anti-racism educational practitioner. To be an anti-racism educator is to be a theorist and a practitioner for social change. Perhaps the task may be easier if it is remembered that the anti-racism educator must always practise what is preached and, conversely, preach what is practised. It is important to fuse the theoretical discourse of anti-racism with the practice of anti-racism organizational change. This means that educators must ground their theoretical discussions about oppression in the harsh, lived realities and experiences of all oppressed peoples. This calls for political and community engagement on the part of anti-racism educators. They need to pursue meaningful change in schools, homes and workplaces to promote the values of equity, fairness and justice. This requires that schools and other institutional organizations learn to critically engage each of their membership in a collective endeavour of power-sharing. Such power-sharing recognizes the individual dignity and collective worth of those participating, and accords everyone a space to be heard and to articulate their dreams. There should be no resistance to individual and collective struggles to have access to the valued goods and services of society. A re-evaluation of what is worthwhile would seem to be part of our collective struggle, too.

Anti-racism calls for putting power relations at the centre of the discourse on race and social difference. It seeks to centre critiques of the (discretionary) use of power and privilege in discussions about race identity and social difference, and how historically constituted relations of domination and subordination are embedded in institutional structures of society. Race, class and gender and their intersections are explored as both sites and sources of difference and identity as well as sites of relations of domination, exploitation and oppression. While the notion of culture(s) and cultural differences are relevant to anti-racism discourse, it stresses that a romanticized notion of culture, which fails to critically interrogate power, is severely limited in the understanding of social reality.

Anti-racism also moves beyond a narrow preoccupation with individual prejudices and discriminatory actions to examine the ways that racist ideas and individual actions are entrenched and (un)consciously supported in institutional structures (Simmons 1994: 27; E. Lee 1994). It is understood in anti-racism discourse that racist practices do not require intentionality, but that such practices are deemed racist in terms of their effects (Anthias and Yuval-Davis 1992: 13).

Following the pioneering works of Canadian educators and social activists Barb Thomas (1984) and Enid Lee (1985), below I have put forward ten basic and interrelated principles of anti-racism education. I believe these principles need to be emphasized in the pursuit of an anti-racism strategy in the context of Canadian schooling. It should be noted that these principles are not presented here in any ranked or hierarchical order, and that additional principles may be articulated by others as there are diverse visions of anti-racism education. What follows here is a discussion of philosophical viewpoints and values governing the pursuit of anti-racism education in Canadian contexts.

The *first* principle of anti-racism education recognizes the social effects of "race," despite the concept's lack of scientific basis. The concept of race is central to anti-racism discourse as a tool for community and academic political organizing for social change. There are powerful social meanings to race which are anchored, particularly, in the lived experiences of minority groups in White-dominated societies. Some people contest the social meaning of race as part of ongoing political attempts to deny racism exists as a set of ideological and material practices which serve to differentiate and discriminate among social groups. In the post-modern context, the notion of race may also be contested on the basis of issues of representation, identity and identifications (McCarthy and Crichlow 1993). The changing meaning of race and racism as a discourse concerning the body, in terms of how the body is read differently in shifting and complex terrains, has become a convenient ground for challenging the intellectual and political significance of the race concept. Race is also contested through the subtle, and not so subtle, deracializing of texts and discourse, as in the "prevailing ideologies and educational practices underlying elite discourse in general" (Dijk 1993: 196). As Troyna also argues, at times there is a deliberate omission in texts of the implications of race and ethnicity and, "more importantly, [an omission of] racism from the interpretive and analytical frames found in academic discourses" (1994: 326). These developments serve to hinder further investigation of historical and contemporary inequities and the importance of instituting progressive anti-racism policies for social change.

Admittedly, key concepts like race and racism, so central to the discourse of anti-racism education, are themselves usually subjected to different interpretations and analyses. As Samuels (1991: 2) points out, this is usually the case with conceptual and analytical categories which are themselves social categories. However, educators cannot overlook the fact that the theoretical exercise of debating the intellectual validity of these concepts can be painful for individuals who live the experiences being conceptualized. As one of my students pointed out in my graduate course on The Sociology of Race and Ethnic Relations, when academics engage in such theoretical exercises, they would do well to remember that they are talking about people's actual lived experiences of being violated, constrained and dominated.

The *second* anti-racism education principle teaches that one cannot understand the full social effects of race without a comprehension of the intersections of all forms of social oppression, including how race is mediated with other forms of social difference. Anti-racism discourse must incorporate gender, class and sexuality as fundamental and relational aspects of the human experience that intersect both in the historical and contemporary reality of people's lives (Leah 1995: 2). This principle is taken up in more detail in Chapter Four when the notion of "integrative anti-racism" is introduced.

The *third* principle questions White (male) power and privilege and the rationality for dominance in society. McIntosh (1990), Thomas (1994), Sleeter (1994) and Dines (1994) point out that often Whiteness, and the privilege of white skin, is taken for granted by many White people. In fact, Gail Dines argues that the "power of Whiteness as a social identity [can be] rendered invisible by privilege (1994: 28). Weiler (1988) shows how power and privilege work together in mutually reinforcing ways to construct social reality for groups in society. I support Weiler's contention that there are powerful societal forces which continually shape the limits of what is possible. There are enormous social, political and economic benefits that historically have accrued, and continue to accrue, to certain individuals in society due to the dominance of White (male) power. It is how economic, political and social power was amassed historically and utilized by certain individuals and groups in society to deny and denigrate the humanity of others that has given rise to the anti-racism struggle. Anti-racism interrogates White privilege and the ideology that maintains and supports both Whiteness as a social identity and the dominant institutions of society. The interrogation of Whiteness can, and should be, an entry point for members of dominant groups in society to join the anti-racism debate (see Frankenberg 1993a, b)

Among the questions that can be examined by White anti-racism educators are: How is Whiteness delineated and read in the schools and in the wider society? Why is White culture so dominant that some students are led to think that Whites are in the majority in the world? Contemporary anti-racism critique of White privilege and power is conditioned by the historical processes of European enslavement, colonization, (mis)representations and (mis)capturings of knowledge about the human condition of indigenous, non-Western peoples. These historical processes are at the centre of the anti-racism examination of political, economic and cultural relations between, and among, social groups in contemporary Euro-Canadian/American society. By questioning institutionalized White power and its basis for dominance in schools, for example, the political and academic project of anti-racism is seeking to rupture how social power and knowledge is shared in contemporary Canadian society. It ought to be asked why the norms, values, ideas, perspectives and traditions of one social group should be adopted as standard by the institutions of society.

Anti-racism education recognizes the relative power and privilege positions of all members of society. But the focus is on institutionalized power and the systemic forces of society that contain a reservoir of privilege for White (heterosexual) males, in particular, to freely tap into. The idea that all peoples have power can trivialize the critiques of hegemonic power. Thus, recognition of the relativity of power is important because, for example, while Black males and females may have access to power and privilege in varied and different settings, such power is constrained and made possible within the parameters and confines of a White-dominated society. It is also in the context of an understanding of how institutionalized power works in a White-dominated society that I use the notion of hegemony. Institutionalized power should be distinguished from social agency. It is power that makes a difference in people's lives which, after all, should be the prime consideration. Power is a pre-eminently social concept. Individual agency as such is tied to and constrained by institutional power. At the same time individuals do have the power to make choices within structures of power. For example, all sports have rules (i.e., structured definitions of action, power and control). However, in playing games players constantly (but not always consciously) "break" or "bend" the rules. They do things which are not permissible within the structure of the rules: they have agency. But that agency has limits, too. One still has to act within the rules (institutional structure) to be recognized as participating in the game. The breaking of the rules is always already available within institutional power structures and creates the possibility for change. As noted above, it is important that power be understood in relational terms, rather than as a fixed quantity. Belkhir, Griffith, Sleeter and Allsup (1994) point out that power is infinite, and sharing it multiplies it. To share power does not necessarily mean to have less power, if social power is read as complementary and enabling in human relations. Particularly for members of the dominant group, recognition of how institutional power works in society should be matched by a recognition of personal gain and benefit. As a corollary, the recognition of privilege should be matched by a recognition of social disadvantage and a willingness to do something about such disadvantage.

The *fourth* principle of anti-racism education—integral to the third—problematizes the marginalization of certain voices in society and, specifically, the delegitimation of the knowledge and experience of subordinated groups in the education system. To speak about power in the anti-racism discourse is to speak also about the social construction of knowledge. I am concerned about what has come to be defined as valid knowledge and how such knowledge, and the power that comes with it, is used to negate and devalue the experiences of subordinated groups. Anti-racism critiques the Euro-Canadian/American dominance of both what constitutes valid knowledge and how such knowledge should be produced and disseminated internally and internationally.

Anti-racism teaching and pedagogy engages the different and multiple ways of knowing in our world in order to advance the course of social knowledge. Educators and students come to know about themselves and society in different ways. Students, for example, have different ways of approaching learning. One approach to teaching and learning cannot meet the needs of all students. Schools, therefore, have to constantly reflect on their teaching methodologies (both in terms of pedagogy and curriculum strategies) to ensure that they capture the wide body of community and off-school knowledge and expertise that students bring to the school and classroom environments (see Erickson 1987; Banks 1993; Ernst, Statzner and Trueba 1994). Schools stand to gain by seeking the assistance of community members with extensive cultural knowledge of the school's student population. This may require a renegotiation of the existing professional definitions of the teacher and a redrawing of the boundaries of knowledge production, interrogation and dissemination.

Anti-racism calls for creating spaces for everyone, but particularly for marginal voices to be heard. It calls for dominant groups in society to listen to the voices of subordinated groups. This is possible if educators can create spaces for alternative and oppositional knowledges to flourish in schools. Dominant groups in society must see that social criticisms made by alienated youth regarding the structures of schooling are well-intentioned. Critiques of the current processes of schooling challenge educators, administrators, students, parents and communities to work more collaboratively and in genuine, power-sharing partnerships to make schools fair for everyone, as well as responsive to societal needs and concerns. The task of anti-racism educators is to create safer spaces for all students to be able to develop some solutions to social problems. Anti-racism education must accord youths the right to utilize their own creativity and resourcefulness to respond to pressing contemporary issues.

The *fifth* principle of anti-racism education is that every form of education must provide for a holistic understanding and appreciation of the human experience, comprising social, cultural, political, ecological and spiritual aspects (see Leah 1995). Anti-racism education teaches about the importance of human co-existence with our environment. To do so, educators must imbue in their students the importance of collective responsibility in relation to upholding the virtues of the social and natural worlds. The effectiveness of such teaching rests with centring the ideas of human spirituality and humane values in the learning process. The notion of spirituality I am employing is quite broad and includes dominant and marginalized concepts of religiosity, faith and religious practice. My conception also includes spiritualities which are not necessarily tied to organized religions or spiritual practices. Rather, it is a connection between the mind, body and soul. By focusing on the spiritual and social development of the individual, anti-racism education supports the development of the necessary grounding and individual confidence from which to work for purposeful change. The individual must develop a deep understanding of the conscious self and how this self relates to others. Change must start from within the individual self. In other words, personal healing is a vital component of political change (see hooks 1993).

The connection between the inner self and the external (social) conditionalities is of utmost concern to the anti-racism struggle for change. Undoubtedly, change is easily understood and probably welcome when individuals and groups experience some positive connection with the vision of society that is being advocated. Individuals and groups must believe that they have the spiritual will and power to usher in change. Anti-racism education seeks to draw connections between the individual self and the community in a manner that allows the self to be grounded in a collective consciousness. The development of a spiritual consciousness arising out of a collective consciousness is to me fundamental to the progressive politics of anti-racism change. In this context, transformative change becomes an embodied and purposeful change. It becomes part of what we are and/or are striving to be. Whether as individuals or as a collective, we carry such change with us in our daily social actions.

The *sixth* principle of anti-racism education focuses on an explication of the notion of "identity," and how identity is linked with/to schooling. Anti-racism education recognizes that students do not go to school as "disembodied" generic youths. Therefore, it is important for educators to understand how students' racial, class, gender, disabilities and sexual identities affect and are affected by the schooling processes and learning outcomes. "Identity," in this context, refers to the individual self and personhood. However, anti-racism education avoids the over-simplification of the individual self which ignores the significant issue of how the inner self is connected to the outer self. Identity cannot be defined in isolation. As Martin (1995: 6) shows, identity acquires its meaning from what it is not, that is, from the "other." Identity implies both uniqueness (selfhood) and sameness (relations with/to others). To determine an identity, one must be perceived to be identical to, or identified with someone else and, at the same time, exhibit some uniqueness. The identity of the self involves more than the individual and it is important for educators to understand how issues of individual and group cultural identities intersect. To claim an identity is a political act which both includes and excludes one's self and "others." Schools themselves construct students in an identity politics by claiming all in their jurisdiction as "students." This closure of identities ignores gender, race and class, thus creating an erasure

Anti-Racism Education

of sexism, racism and classism: "We're all the same. It's what's inside that counts."

Anti-racism education links identity with schooling in different ways in order to give meaning, place, context, origin and history to discussions of who we are, as teachers, administrators, students, parents and members of a community. Students, like any other group, articulate multiple, overlapping and shifting identities. One task of anti-racism teaching is to help students make connections between their own self and the group they comprise. Furthermore, most students are engaged in individual and collective struggles to identify with the education system, that is, with the classroom teaching methods, the learning materials, and the general school environment. "Why or how is this relevant to me?" students often ask from multiple social locations. Another anti-racism challenge, therefore, is for schools to develop a more critical understanding of how the varied identities of students and teachers affect the processes of schooling and ways of knowing, teaching, learning and understanding the world. In sum, the notion of identity is intertwined with the processes of knowledge production.

Race identity formation and the associated struggles at both individual and collective levels are part of critical anti-racism discourse. Questions of identity are brought to the fore in part because race still remains "a fundamental principle of social organization and identity formation" (Omi and Winant 1993: 5); to be without racial identity in a racialized society is "to be in danger of having no identity" (Anthias and Yuval-Davis 1992: 50). The fact that there are "constantly shifting parameters through which race is understood" (Omi and Winant 1993: 6) and that, as Le Camp (1995) argues, pressure from the dominant sector of society requires that all members of the society identify themselves as part of specific racial/ethnic groups only serves to highlight the significance of the notion of identity in the anti-racism discourse.[1] Positionality does not only require that everyone determine their location; it also requires that we all are able to define who we are. For many, this is indeed a big challenge.

New racial identities are being constructed in post-modern society, raising a series of questions anti-racism education must seek answers to a series of questions around narratives of social identities. For example, as Omi and Winant ask: "How are group interests assigned in society? How is social and political status ascribed? How are social roles performed? How is human agency attained" (1993: 6)? Within Euro-Canadian/American schooling contexts, the social construction of "Blackness" and "Whiteness" has serious implications for the schooling and education of all students, but particularly for students of African descent. To clarify, Black/African youths live in a society where they are constantly bombarded with representational stereotypes of their "true" identity. Take a look at most of the television shows in which there are Blacks, either they are in trouble with the law or involved in some form of illicit activity. Where else are the youths of a race predicted to be failures, based on the crimes of certain individuals of the same race? The expectation that Black youths will fail,

32

especially in the so-called hard sciences, means most of these youths find themselves being channelled into "technical" or "vocational" classes. So, given the (mis)representation of Black youths in the print/visual media, plus their lived experiences, is it any wonder that they are faced with these dilemmas? Rarely, if ever, do Black youths get a positive or true representation of what their reality is about. The issue of how students link their identity and their schooling is important to understanding the causes of student disengagement from school. Students can engage the power of human agency to name and define themselves for collective action and to articulate an emancipatory discourse. An anti-racism education creates the possibility of students using this ability. The power of self and group definitions allows some students to recognize their individual and group ancestry and cultural heritage as powerful sources of knowledge. These sources provide a basis from which to challenge their historic marginality in the school system. In such a situation, the margin becomes a site of resistance to the powerful political, economic, cultural and educational forces of Euro-Canadian/ American hegemony (see Ibrahim 1994; Solomon 1992).

The *seventh* principle of anti-racism education acknowledges the pedagogic need to confront the challenge of diversity and difference in Canadian society. It recognizes the urgent need for an education system that is more inclusive and is capable of responding to minority concerns about public schooling. The idea of inclusive schooling sees schools as "working communities" in that the powerful notions of "community" and "social responsibility" are brought from the margins into the centre of the processes of delivering education. Today, it is tempting to say "no one knows what community means anymore." But surely, "community" must mean something. The notion of schools as "working communities" means that schools should teach the values fundamental to a working community. Schools should seek peaceful co-existence among students, teaching staff, school administrators, parents and local communities through instilling mutual respect, collective work and collective responsibility. Schools must genuinely and unequivocally value the experiences of every member of this more inclusive community. Diversity and difference mean a wealth of knowledge is available for the benefit of all. Consequently, schooling and education must proceed from the understanding that everyone in school has something to offer, and that diverse viewpoints, experiences and perspectives should be heard and valued. Good education progresses by critically sharing all available knowledges. Anti-racism pedagogy does not seek to nullify power and social difference; it recognizes that everyone speaks from places which have real power differences. It makes these differences into a resource. Often, this results in a situation where the less powerful are educating the more powerful.

Inclusive schools respond to the needs and challenges of diversity in their education of the youth by tapping into the cultural knowledge of parents, guardians and community workers. Such schools take the initiative and set out to break the false separation between the *school* and the *community*. But the idea of inclusive educational practice means a sharing of power on the basis of the diversity and difference manifested in the school body. This includes dealing with questions of representation, that is, the active recruitment, retention and promotion of minority staff and teachers. The mere representation of a range of ethnocultural differences among staff and teachers should help students' identification with the school, and also help respond to the question of power-sharing. This is particularly important since students see teachers as occupying positions of power and influence. An inclusive representation of differences will also engage the rich experiences, perspectives and viewpoints that are brought into the school.

A genuinely inclusive school also ensures that school curriculum is taught from an anti-racism perspective that makes a conscious and determined effort to centre individual and group experiences and cultures in students' learning. Diversity is not seen as the problem, but rather as how schools and institutions relate to difference. Inclusive schools cultivate sustained institutional support for the development of minority students' cultures, events and interests (see Dei and Razack 1995).

The *eighth* principle of anti-racism education acknowledges the traditional role of the education system in producing and reproducing not only racial, but also gender, sexual and class-based inequalities in society. Schools are part of the institutional structure sanctioned by society and the state. The public school system, in particular, has historically served the material, political and ideological interests of the state and those of industrial capital. The public school is a site for the production and reproduction of the ideological hegemony of the state and of the economic interests of global capital (Ng 1993a, b). A critical anti-racism discursive framework helps us understand the nature of the interaction existing between the labour demands of the ruthlessly competitive global economy and the processes of schooling that accord differential treatment and educational outcomes for students of diverse racial and economic backgrounds. The structures of public schooling continually serve to segment the labour force by systematically consigning students certain social categories or classes. For example, working-class students are still streamed into vocational schools and, subsequently, manual labour (Curtis, Livingstone and Smaller 1992). Black students are "pushed out" (Dei, Holmes, Mazzuca, McIsaac and Campbell 1995) into unforgiving and exploitative job markets. This consignment of students may be described as naturalized through various ideological practices within the structures and institutions of schooling. The resultant inequalities among students, as they negotiate the processes of schooling, become constituted in the idea of student "success" or "failure." These inequalities are also consequential in that they offer a supply of workers who are separated hierarchically. This is not necessarily acknowledged in popular discourses constructed around individualized notions of "student success" and "student failures." Unfortunately, "meritocracy" still has a central place in educational practice and theory.

Basic Principles of Anti-Racism Education

Programs must be put in place to target students marginalized on these bases, because research continually shows that education has historically not worked for all students (Curtis, Livingstone and Smaller 1992).

The *ninth* principle of anti-racism education stresses that the school problems experienced by the youth cannot be understood in isolation from the material and ideological circumstances in which the students find themselves. Current national and global economic restructuring has serious implications for Canadian schooling, particularly for racial minority, women and economically disadvantaged youths. Many youths experience the strains and stresses of family breakdown and abuse, and economic deprivation in a job-scarce economy. They live in a very competitive, individualistic world which is, at times, very uncompromising with individuals who are deemed by dominant ruling groups to be a burden on the social safety net. Look, for example, at the "workfare" policies that are being considered and put in place by Canadian and American governments. Increasingly, marginalized people will actually be competing to get work which will be tied to their social welfare payments of various kinds. Definitions of success in life are very narrow and are for the most part individually centred. Society is quick to blame youths when things do not go as expected for them. Therefore we need to regularly ask, "Whose expectations?" Explanations for social decadence and deviance that highlight the underlying systemic and material causes for youth transgressions are often hurriedly dismissed as a calculated attempt to absolve transgressors of individual culpability. For example, youths who drop out of school are personally blamed and quickly characterized as irresponsible (Dei, Holmes, Mazzuca, McIsaac and Campbell 1995). But many of these youths aspire to lead a good and decent life. They have dreams like everyone else. Is it in the nature of these youths to simply "fail" or are there significant material and ideological circumstances that should be taken into account? The search for explanations for some students' non-conformity to the dominant values, norms and values of society demands a holistic analysis of the social, political and economic structuralization of society.

The *tenth* and related principle of anti-racism questions pathological explanations of the "family" or "home environment" as a source of the "problems" some youth experience in relation to schooling. Such explanations only serve to divert attention away from a critical analysis of the institutional structures within which the delivery of formal education takes place. As many critical educators have pointed out, in order to justify the status quo, conventional modes of thought tend to mystify and/or reify social reality by attributing causal priority for "failure" to factors within the victims themselves. Denying and/or shifting responsibility for school failures avoids a critical interrogation of what happens in schools and why, how students experience schools and why, and how this experience affects their learning outcomes and/or conventional definitions of school "success" and "failure" (see McLaren 1993).

Anti-racism education teaches that schools should be promoting effective student-teacher-parent-community interactions, rather than pathologizing families and students and blaming victims for socio-historical and structural injustices. There must be effective processes put in place for communication and interactions with parents and community groups. Parents should not simply be plugged into schools; they should share in the vital decision-making processes affecting the administrative control of schools, along with administrators, teachers and students. They must be part of the process of (re)writing school curriculum (both official and hidden) to ensure that all viewpoints are presented. There is also an urgent need for institutional support for students, families, teachers and administrators dealing with the racism, poverty and unemployment that affect schooling and learning outcomes.

In effect, anti-racism education contextualizes current academic knowledge about differential educational outcomes for diverse youths. It recognizes how economic and political conditionalities mediate micro- and macro-level experiences of youths and families and of their local communities. For example, economic measures such as the retrenchment of workers and the reduction in budgetary deficits through cutbacks to social services and transfer payments to schools negatively impact on the ability of some families today to provide a supportive educational environment to their children. It is not that these parents want to shed adult responsibilities for educating the youth. There is much to be learned from an understanding of how local communities and groups are responding to global economic changes as these affect schooling and education. Anti-racism education seeks to bring economic issues into the debate on educational reform for social and transformative change.

The above principles of anti-racism education provide educators with significant guidelines for working for educational change. A very seductive and dangerous approach for an educator to take is one in which she or he views and understands social reality from a deficit model/paradigm. This danger is more pronounced in the anti-racism educational project. A theoretical approach to anti-racism work, which begins with the educational premise that "you have less, therefore you need this" or "I have it, and therefore you learn from me" can be very disempowering and may easily derail any transformative potential in anti-racism work. It is important to remember what Hunter (1983: 243) cautioned against: the belief that one's own reality is the only reality worth speaking about can be the most dangerous of all delusions. We must also advise against the failure to acknowledge what things are good for, without necessarily having to attribute everything to a particular event. All social experiences have histories and are situated in a shifting complex of power relations. To claim one experience as definitive potentially negates and diminishes other experiences. Educators, therefore, must recognize what anti-racism is good for, what it can do and any possible limitations of the discourse.

Educators' acknowledgement of their own intellectual and experiential limits points to the ways in which "difference" (McCarthy 1990) operates to define us all. Educators' difference from their students is not simply based on age.

Basic Principles of Anti-Racism Education

Understanding the notion of "difference" is significant to the anti-racism debate. Anti-racism education should be able to explore how difference is named, lived, experienced, imagined and acknowledged in the lives of students, teachers, parents and the local communities. For educators, the issue really is how they treat and relate to human and social differences in the classroom. Anti-racism must define, conceptualize and perceive "difference" from the standpoint of those who occupy the margins of society and continually have to resist their marginality through collective action. For example, an educator's understanding of how an off-school marginalized community sees social difference as implicating their life chances in society is a useful pedagogical tool in teaching about social oppression and inequality.

The question is, how do we teach difference? Difference must be taught in a way that allows people to acquire the strength to work collectively for transformative change. Difference should be taught in a manner that recognizes our individual and collective strengths. Difference should not be taught in a manner that renders exotic and romanticizes the "other." We recognize our difference in order to learn from each other. We must also recognize the difference that makes a difference (Derrida 1978), or the difference that differences make (see also Britzman 1993). Furthermore, it is simply not enough for an educator to teach, and for students to learn, about other cultures and not engage in a project that unravels the power relations embedded in the construction of knowledge. The anti-racism educator must assist students to learn how the dominant culture systematically skews a critical understanding, acknowledgement and appreciation of marginalized groups in the school system.

A related question concerns the extent to which an emphasis on differences can aid or impede a politics of social transformation. There is little doubt that a politics of similarities can mask forms of social injustice. In an ideal world we could not deny the importance of connecting on the basis of our commonalities. After all, we should be able to "visualize a community" in the midst of difference and diversity. It is important *not to confuse diversity with divisiveness*. However, highlighting or privileging difference, in a manner that engenders divisiveness, is not a virtue of diversity.

What anti-racism education seeks to do is build what have been termed "communities of difference." This task can only be undertaken successfully if educators first learn how to deal with differences and the inherent conflictual interests and power imbalances in our societies. In North America we are still having a difficult time dealing with our differences. We seriously need to listen and learn from each other as part of the challenge of working across differences. We should be able to move beyond the mere acknowledgement of "difference" and deal with the fundamental issues of distribution of power and privilege within and among communities. This, no doubt, will only be possible if anti-racism education starts with an analysis of social differences (race, class, gender) as sites of exploitation and oppression to deepen our understanding of the human condition and complexity of social reality. Anti-racism must engage the politics of difference recognizing both the diversity of human experiences (see McCarthy 1990; Walcott 1994) and that when a particular experience is universalized it is usually accomplished at the expense of making another experience invisible.

But the challenge, as I see it, is for anti-racism educators to ensure that a politics of difference does not unduly paralyze or compromise a larger transformative project for meaningful social change. It should be possible to develop a politics of transformation that allows us to move collectively while retaining and accepting our differences. There is power in collective action and we must at all times avoid the dangers of internalizing the language of specificities to the extent that we are unable to forge alliances among peoples and groups who share a common vision of social transformation. There is another African proverbial saying that is relevant to forming alliances: "one broomstick is easier to break than the bundle." Anti-racism political organizing for change should be guided by this knowledge.

To engage in effective anti-racism work also requires knowledge of how to deal with resistance (although this term has multiple and contradictory definitions). Anti-racism educators should not be afraid of, or be paralyzed by, resistance. Educators have to be able to deal with the everyday opposition and resistance to anti-racism issues in the schools. Critical educators should be able to identify both the *moment* and the *allies* for anti-racism work. They should be able to identify how schools, through institutionalized practices, cultivate/nurture hegemonic ideologies for the entrenchment of the status quo. Educators must be able to locate the sources of disempowerment of marginalized students in the convenient "blame-the-victim" approach and/or the "culture-deficit" model of understanding societal problems. As Enid Lee has repeatedly warned, resisting racism and social oppression is having the courage to say both what one is in favour of, as well as what one is against (1993).

Dealing with resistance and opposition to anti-racism is to engage in a political project to challenge the false distinction between the so-called defenders of academic excellence and quality education on the one hand and the promoters of diversity and educational equity on the other. The issues of diversity, excellence, quality and equity in education are inseparable.

Anti-racism classroom teaching must stress the relevance of what is taught and learned to the material conditions of everyday existence of all members of society. Anti-racism educators should be prepared to engage in issues-oriented teaching; to teach about race, social difference and resistance; to recognize and deal with social oppression and institutionalized and global inequalities; and to act conscientiously to install a more just social order.

Note

1. This is one of the tools and problems of dichotomous conceptions of social relations and identities. People are forced into either/or categories, while in practice we are both/and. For example, Canadian passports say "Canadian Citizen" not "French-Canadian" or "African-Canadian" or "White Anglo-Canadian." Any splitting of the category of "Canadian" is not institutionally sanctioned, despite the reality that "Canadians" are Canadian and Aboriginal, Canadian and French, Canadian and White Anglo, Canadian and African.

Chapter Three
Theoretical Approaches to the Study of Race

Given that race is central to critical anti-racism studies, it is important for us to understand both the historical and contemporary ideological and material meanings of the race concept. This chapter explores how race knowledge and racism have been, and continue to be, interrogated, understood, produced and reproduced. Certain questions are paramount to the discussion. For example, how do we understand the significance of the shift in the meanings and interpretations of race; how have the purely biologistic racial theories of the past come to be replaced by the socio-historical constructions of the present? What accounts for the persistence of discredited race thinking in modern society? Do changing material conditions give rise to changes in racial ideology (Omi and Winant 1993: 4)? Even as we engage in this discussion we continually need to remind ourselves that the social practice of racism is the problem and not the theoretical conceptions of race per se (see James 1995).

There has been much scholarly discussion on the origins of the race concept and how the concept manifests its significance in the everyday practices of society. In fact, numerous academic essays continue to broach the subject of race and racisms, each offering valuable insights to our understanding of the social, ideological and biological constructions and abstract formations of race, and of the practice of racism in society (see Cox 1976; West 1987; Miles 1989; Goldberg 1993; Omi and Winant 1993, 1994; Banks 1994a; Rattansi and Westwood 1994). This chapter does not reiterate the many well established critical arguments and ideas concerning race and racism. Rather, I focus briefly on the theoretical arguments through which the race concept has historically been understood, articulated and acted upon in world histories.

Notwithstanding the difficulty inherent in talking about the origins of the race concept, I contend that the idea of race may have been an essential feature of early societal formations, especially as individuals searched for social explanations for the nature and consequences of human differences. Still, the origins of the race concept can appropriately be tied to Western European philosophical and belief systems and, particularly, to their colonial and imperial expansion activities in the seventeenth century (Reynolds and Lieberman 1993). Some writers put this date at around the sixteenth century (see Goldberg 1993). Race, at the time, was a powerful and useful concept for sorting out the human variations observed by European explorers, conquerors and colonizers. As Reynolds and Lieberman (1993) argue, a self-righteous racial ideology was developed to legitimize the ruthless exploitation and subjugation of non-Western people. Since the seventeenth century, the race concept has been applied, to varying degrees, by social and natural scientists in the course of everyday reasoning and research about human social relations and interactions (Miles 1989).

But what meaning does race carry in contemporary society? As already pointed out, it is a socially constructed category which lacks any sound scientific validity. Yet race continues to gain in social currency because of its utility in distributing unequal power, privilege and social prestige (see Henry, Tator, Mattis and Rees 1995). It has become an effective tool for determining the distribution of rewards, penalties and punishments. The concept has been used to "divide and rule" peoples, a practice that is itself assisted by the human desire and craze to categorize and classify individuals and social groups. Together with other aspects and dimensions of our individual and collective identities, race continually implicates how we, as humans, come to know, see, understand and interpret ourselves and our world.

Consequently, *race matters* in human lives and social interactions. The brutal facts of economic history and the harsh realities of contemporary society clearly demonstrate there is, and has always been, an ideological meaning to race. This is apparent in spite of the fact that social scientists, and particularly early researchers on race, acknowledge the difficulty of defining and operationalizing the race concept. The problem was, and continues to be, the lack of clarity and the intellectual danger of using conceptual and analytical categories that are themselves social constructs. Such analytical concepts tend to gain materiality and replace and obscure the original focus.

Historically, disagreements among social scientists have rotated around two issues: firstly, the number of races into which human groups can be classified, and the criteria for such classification is debated; and secondly, there is disagreement among another group of social scientists who argue that there is no such thing as race. They assume that it is not possible to "properly" identify the race of a given group or individual because of historical migration and "interracial mixing (Reynolds and Lieberman 1993: 110–14). This position is a step forward, but leaves race in place as an essential category of human identities and bodies, and it is unable to account for the political and social production of racialized difference. In spite of this research which unequivocally states that it is not possible to categorize humans based on race, some contemporary "scientists" continue to propagate atrocious ideas about the nature and ability of different races. We still have to contend with the Rushtons of the world and the notion of the "bell curve." Some "reputable" scientists continue to use their privilege and freedom to serve the cause of the racist, fascist Right.[1] Today, questions surrounding the taxonomic validity of racial categories and the arbitrariness of the race concept have been superseded by discussions about the materiality of race as a social, ideological and political category in human social life. To understand some of these earlier conceptualizations of race we need to examine the ideas espoused in early racial discourses. In this exercise, we must ask, for example, how has the race concept been constructed historically both in the biological and social sense?

Historically, several conceptual and analytical frameworks have been developed to buttress forms of racist thinking and academic discourses, as well as the economic and social power of certain groups in society. These ideas have spanned from the conception of race as a purely biological category to the social construction of race in the material and ideological conditions of society (regarding the latter, see Banton 1967; Miles 1989; Figueroa 1991; Anthias and Yuval-Davis 1992; Omi and Winant 1994). Early race analysis was rooted and produced in the interest of scientific justification of human oppression, exploitation and slavery. In the biological sense, the race concept was based on a categorization of people on the basis of perceived differences in intelligence levels. One justification by European scientists for the enslavement of African peoples was that they were, it was believed, a "sub-human" species, like cattle. They supposedly did not have the "same" capacities for language, communication and culture as their European oppressors. Most of this discourse arose out of the "neutral, rational science" of biology. In its social conception, the term "race" was/is argued to be a social, political and ideological construct. Notwithstanding the fact that there are still important forces in society who argue for biological differences and intelligence, the current strength of the social meaning of race rests on the understanding that the concept cannot be defined biologically. Rather, as many have pointed out, race is a product of specific socio-historical and political contexts (see Omi and Winant 1994). Goldberg recently wrote about the "different racisms in the same place at different times; or different racisms in various different places at the same time" (1993: 91).

Race is now widely seen as a social relational category. One of the prominent bases of contemporary definitions of race is a focus on socially selected physical characteristics (see Wilson 1973: 6). While this definition of race as a social construct based on perceived phenotypical differences is generally accepted, it is important also to acknowledge the historical power of the dominant to define and categorize human populations. An example is the European colonialists' misnaming of so-called North-American "Indians." The asymmetrical power relations between dominant and subordinate groups in societies in general have been instrumental in the production and dissemination of particular race knowledges, both nationally and internationally.

Biddiss (1979) points out that the development of racial theories was central to the dominant ideas of European bourgeois civilization and aesthetics (e.g., ideas of intelligence, character, physical prowess and beauty). Eighteenth and nineteenth century ideas reified the concept of race within a theoretical framework of biological determinism. Connections were made between supposedly scientific and mystical approaches to race. Racial ideas were presented as pseudo-religious thought, and later were adapted to a more secularized society (Biddiss 1979). In fact, the role of the Church in maintaining a race differentiation through definitions of "unChristian," "savage and unholy practices" in European expansion was paramount during these periods. For many scholars of the time, what was worth stressing was the importance of racial biology for maintaining and justifying oppressive human and social relations. Racial typologies were devised to categorize humans on the basis of perceived phenotypical differences with the understanding and implication that there was little hope for changes in "racially different behavioural models" (Macchiusi 1993: 60). Education and socio-environmental forces and structures were denied any significant role in the politics of social and global transformation. Racial typologies, buttressed by a Eurocentric view of the world, were critical in justifying European practices of cultural, economic and political genocide of non-European peoples. As Macchiusi (1993: 50) additionally points out, in the biological formulation of racist doctrines, the oversimplification of race and racialism in biological facts also denied the role of human agency.

The failure and the inability to conceive of race relations as ostensibly power relations—relations of domination and subordination—prevented any critical discussion about human resistance and agency in their diverse emotional, symbolic, physical, intellectual and social forms (see Foucault 1980). Eighteenth and nineteenth century race theorists simply adopted biologically determinist and essentialist positions in the discourse on race and racism. This fermented the development of the binary oppositions of "us" and "them," which undermined the formation of a progressive social movement for change.[2]

Among the popular nineteenth century theoretical/scientific perspectives on race, human relations and society were the views of social Darwinists, early socio-biologists, eugenicists, structural functionalists and socio-psychologists. *Social Darwinism* is a theory about the "survival of the fittest" applied to human groups. Social Darwinism is characterized by a mode of evolutionary thinking which applies biology and biological analogies to the study and analysis of human social relations and cultural organization. As Banton (1977: 89–100) points out, early social Darwinist thinking on race extends the philosophy of evolution and biological development of animals to humans and the development of societies. Throughout the late nineteenth century, social Darwinism provided a conceptual framework for (scientific) racial thinking, arguing that the nature of human societies and cultural development is a product of evolutionary forces. This idea was conceived on the application of biological and physical principles of evolution to the understanding of how different races adapted socially through the process of competitive survival. Social Darwinists challenge the idea of permanent racial types, arguing that as humans compete with one another for survival, one group (race) will eventually win the struggle. The victorious group (race), so it is rationalized, achieves its success because of the group's inherent superiority over other races. As Miles contends, social Darwinists believed that "there was a struggle for survival among different human 'races,' in the course of which those with lesser intelligence or capacity for 'civilization' would eventually disappear, their elimination being evidence of their natural inability to evolve" (1989: 36–7). Such thinking is not only racist but also serves to justify the inhumane treatment of people who are perceived to be different from the dominant group. Further, it supports the idea that aggression, dominance and competition are desirable human characteristics.

The *socio-biological* perspective of the nineteenth century borrows many of the ideas of social Darwinists. It conceptualizes race as an important biological component of human social relationships. The focus is on using biology to explain the basis of human social co-operation. Race is seen as a primordial feature (see van den Berghe 1985). It is argued that relations among human groups (race relations) are governed by primordial attachments, rather than material calculations of economic advantage. The socio-biological view of race is essentially informed by a theory of human nature which argues that humans have innate preferences to associate with members of their "own kind." A more sociological critique of this paradigm of race relations is that interactions among human groups in society are not simply based on friendly associations, but on issues of material, economic and political advantage, necessity, opportunity and convenience.

Borrowing from these early biological interpretations of race and social relations, *eugenicists* developed racist ideas which sought to link race and intelligence and to establish a theory informed by the notion of the genetically inherited mental inferiority of certain groups in society. It is argued that essentially biological features determining race (note the direction of reasoning) also determine both individual's and a group's mental, social, political and cultural capabilities and capacities. Eugenicists focus on the genetics of race to explain human social differences. Such views provide additional arguments in support of later conceptions of innate-difference theories based on supposedly scientific, culture-free intelligence testing. It is enthused that physical and mental characteristics can be correlated and that both are passed on from one generation to another by hereditary factors. This is argued in spite of the first law of statistics which emphasizes that correlation does not determine causality nor is statistical significance the same as social significance. The White race is assumed superior to all others.

It is important to recognize the power of eugenicist thinking. The ultimate inhumanity of genocide, as in such highly reprehensible practices as human enslavement and the Holocaust, is without any doubt linked to such biological definitions of race. Social oppression and inequality among groups is also blamed by eugenicists on factors and causes within oppressed groups. Genetic interpretations are offered for observable discrepancies in intelligence scores of different races. These interpretations also became powerful "scientific" justifications and ideological rationales for the inhumane treatment of groups perceived to be "different" from the dominant. As many have pointed out, such ideological reasoning served to justify the status quo by attributing causal priority to the victims themselves.

Structural functionalism, as a sociological theoretical perspective, focuses on a description of the structures and functions of society and its institutions, rather than an explication of the origins and implications of cultural differences and similarities. Human society is viewed as a biological organism with interrelated and interdependent parts which are integrated to form a harmonious whole. Dominant institutions of society are rarely interrogated as sites of power contestation and social contradictions. The structural functionalist paradigm views race and ethnic relations in society as potentially antagonistic and full of conflict. However, as Zine (1994) points out, unlike the contemporary view which holds that conflict is a basic and natural element of the social order, structural functionalist theory views conflict as negative, as posing a threat to the goals of maintaining equilibrium and engaging continuous, regular and controlled change to preserve and improve existing social relations. Like social Darwinists, eugenicists and socio-biologists, structural functionalists wish to preserve existing social relations, and consequently prefer to focus on the contemporary nature of racial and ethnic groups.

Societal policies of assimilation were supported by the view that conflict is disruptive. These policies were designed to ensure racial/ethnic groups' conformity to the status quo. Later ethnographic studies (see Barth 1969) were to show that, rather than assimilation and conformity, the processes of social interaction between racial and ethnic groups did in fact intensify and solidify racial and ethnic identities and conflict. Structural functionalist thought, nevertheless, moves away from purely biological explanations of race and racial types to emphasize social-structural factors and cultural variables as accounting for human differences (see Dollard 1939; Powdermaker 1939; Myrdal 1944).

Much of the writing on race and racial difference employing this theoretical perspective focuses on explanations of contact situations, problems of adjustment, and social interactions among different and diverse human populations (see Cox 1948: 320). It is held that an important aspect of improving social and racial relations is through the strengthening of families and cultures of non-Whites (Lewis 1969, 1975; Moynihan 1965) or through interracial contact. There is little or no critical analysis of the unequal conditions under which different social groups and individuals function in society. The conflict between groups in society over the distribution of wealth, power and resources is hardly problematized. While acknowledging moral tensions in society around issues of fairness and equality, it is felt that the nature and function of the very systems of racial and ethnic stratification will resolve any moral dilemmas, tensions and contradictions, and foster peace and harmony.

Anti-Racism Education

Many of these ideas can be found in current interpretations and/or explanations of how societal events affect students' disengagement and failure at school. The current focus in much educational research is on students' cultures and home backgrounds, rather than on critical interrogation of the structures of schooling and education. Also being propagated in debates are ideas about human nature and the ability of individuals to do what is right for the well-being of society. Current rhetoric from the new Right, particularly in the US, blames all of society's problems on the disintegration of the family and family values.

Socio-psychological approaches to race and racism concede that race relations have little to do with biology. Nevertheless, this perspective underestimates the power of institutional structures to provide a space for individuals in society to discriminate against one another. The classic writings of Adorno, Frenkel-Brunswik, Levinson and Nevitt-Sanford (1950), Allport (1954) and Wellman (1977) make a conceptual distinction between prejudice as an attitude and discrimination as a behaviour or act. The authors problematize individual prejudice, and consequently focus on individual intentions without critically examining the outcomes or social effects of individual prejudicial behaviour. For example, Adorno, Frenkel-Brunswik, Levinson and Nevitt-Sanford (1950) focus on individual prejudice as the outcome of a particular type of personality which, due to child-rearing practices and/or early childhood socialization, tends to be sympathetic to social and political beliefs that are hostile to minority groups (e.g., Blacks, Jews and Catholics). Again, we can find these ideas being freely expressed in our societies today as, for example, when the systemic problem of racism is presented as one of ignorance and individual prejudice. "Banking" theories of education (inadequately) respond to racism in this way.[3] Clearly, not everyone sees racism as a systemic problem that is endemic and is continually reproduced by the very institutions that govern and regulate our lives in society.

But anti-racism is not simply a study of racist intent. It is more a study of racist effect. The study of racism delves into the obvious outcomes, that is, the social consequences and effects of actualizing individual intent, as well as the structural conditions that foster social discrimination. This understanding is left out of socio-psychological approaches to the study of race and racism. Later ideological conceptions of race critically interrogate not only the racist theories that have been passed on as scientific facts, but also the social and institutional practices that systematically deny certain groups access to valued goods and services of society.

Today there are still some crucial racist writers (albeit a few) who pretend to do scholarly work and yet, to use James Banks' words in another context, "view diversity as deviance and difference as deficits" (1993: 6). On the whole, however, very few, if any, truly scholarly contemporary writings argue that race is biologically ordained or that it is a fixed category. In fact, current *ideological* and *stratification* approaches have brought new meanings to race and racisms.

Theoretical Approaches . . .

Many of the current approaches are challenging everyday common-sense racism and "the normal way of doing things" (Essed 1990: 50). Current thinking marks a departure from past perspectives in that race relations are seen primarily as social relations (see Figueroa 1991: 28). That the socio-historical factors of immigration, European conquest and colonization foster racialized ideologies is stressed to show how historical and contemporary social relations have always been race, class and gender-based relations. As Macchiusi points out, "modern concepts of race do not always have to do with phenotypical differences between peoples"; contemporary racism is "a conflation of class, religions, and broad cultural concerns and definitions" (1993: 60). It is also "now possible to perpetuate racial domination without making any explicit reference to race at all" (Omi and Winant 1993: 7–8). Of equal significance, the notion of "ethnicity"— a social relational category defined by socially selected cultural characteristics— has increasingly appeared in contemporary race relations discourse to capture the myriad forms of identity formation to which a simplistic definition of race fails to speak.

Additionally, emerging meanings of race, according to Anthias and Yuval-Davis (1992: 12), denote particular ways in which communal differences come to be constructed. Today, we can speak of culturalist forms of racisms that do not depend on racial typologies (Gilroy 1992; see also Razack 1995a). Current discussions and explications about "culture," "nation" and "heritage" can, and do, become new tropes for producing racialized doctrines and reproducing overtly racist discourses. Within all contemporary societies, cultural differences have become signifiers and/or markers of race, and the bases for racist practice and other forms of social discrimination. One only needs to take a critical look at the code words contained in the speeches of the extreme Right. For example, they portray immigrants and some minorities in Euro-Canadian/American society as cultural laggards, welfare cheats and the primary beneficiaries of affirmative action and other employment equity measures. It is important that we understand how these culturalist forms of racism work. They are evident in the schools when, for example, students' home cultures and families are continually pathologized and blamed for creating "academic deficits" in minority children.

Generally, implicit in both the common-sense and the highly structured understanding of racism is the acknowledgement that it is "a set of postulates . . . which serve to differentiate and dominate" (Anthias and Yuval-Davis 1992: 15). It is clear from modern discourses on race and racism that, besides its saliency, there is more than skin-colour racism. In effect, racism is multi-faceted and cannot be explained away as people's simplistic conceptions of biological differences. The meaning of race continues to change, just as it did in the past. It may be argued that today, in some quarters, "scientific racism" has given way to cultural racism. We can see this in conventional discourses about "international development." African peoples, for example, may no longer be seen as biologically inferior. They may be seen as techno-culturally inadequate (Essed 1990: 14).

47

African countries can be presented in some Western "development" circles as "basket cases" populated by "helpless" peoples. Hence "development" is conceptualized on their behalf. Development is defined in relation to what White, middle-class Westerners perceive African peoples lack and/or what they are expected to become. Local views, conceptions and initiatives about development are discarded because, in the political language of some international development agencies, local peoples have nothing to offer. This approach to development on the continent may not merely be Eurocentric and male-biased, it is also racist (Dei 1994a).

Contemporary writers on critical race studies generally share Omi and Winant's view that race is a "fundamental principle of social organization and identity formation" (1993: 5). Many also share Miles' contention that race is "an ideology, a process of signification and a system of categorization based on a hierarchy of groups" (1989: 84). Banks (1994a) points out that as a social construct, race reflects both objective reality and the subjectivity of the knower. Giroux (1992a: 26) points out that racism "cannot be dealt with in a purely analytical way" and that the race discourse transcends discussions about economics, culture, politics and power. It is about more than a collective historical experience of colonialism and slavery.

These critical interpretations indicate that the concept of race and the social practices of racism should be studied and addressed at both theoretical and experiential levels. Labelling race as a strictly theoretical concept could discredit the claims of those who have been victims of racist practices (see also Purdy 1994). Similarly, engaging in highly abstract discussions of what race is and is not can easily derail a political project. It can undermine those mobilizing to fight the scourge of racism through responses that recognize the historical and contemporary injustices and oppression of individuals and groups in society. This linkage between theory and practice in anti-racism work must be recognized, as the theoretical work and viewpoint are only valid in their interplay with a practice of opposing racism and other forms of social oppression and of fighting for their elimination.

Furthermore, as with theorizations of other forms of oppression, there are dangers of obfuscating the meaning and reality of race and racism (see Bulham 1985: 120–1). This danger is recognized by relatively current (re)conceptualizations of race, as they reject the idea of fixed, immutable categories. As Gilroy (1993a, b), Miles (1989), Gillborn (1995a, b) and many others argue, race is not, and should not be, a homogenous category. Current interpretations also de-mystify and de-emphasize any biological, physical and physiological differences between and among groups. Debates are now generally anchored in a recognition of a strong material, political and ideological base to the race concept that signifies real and imagined differences among and between people.

Unfortunately, not everyone has shied away from a simplistic construction of race as an exclusive, essentialized category. Some still fail to take into account the material realities of people and our complex and varied subjective identities (Train 1995). In such cases, the fact that the everyday material lives and practices of people reveal complex, multiple and changing subject positions and identifications has not been fully recognized. What anti-racism discourse can do is bring new meanings to the notion of race. It can impart powerful social meanings which stress that races are not discrete entities and that race is not synonymous with one class or gender. Anti-racism must be able to propagate new meanings which emphasize and teach that race is not an attribute of minorities only. We must talk about White as a colour and also challenge the fact that "racelessness," to use Fordham's (1988) conception, is a privilege afforded only to Whites (Joyce 1995a).

Anti-racism education must help reject essentialist and reductionist approaches to race analysis (see Gillborn 1995a, b). It must also refute a priori assumptions of White racism that let off the hook intra- and inter-group racisms and non-White racial domination of, and discrimination towards, other minority groups. Both Gillborn (1995a, b) and Greene (1994) have called for moving beyond a simplistic Black–White duality that feeds on binary oppositions and modes of thought. There is also an emerging critique of narrow conceptions of race and conventional anti-racism studies that fail to draw on the globalization of racism. At the same time, anti-racism studies need to take seriously what Britzman (1993) sees as the reframing of race in reaction to an oppressive system, and the implications of this for progressive politics. What emerging critical studies of race and anti-racism can do is concretely ground discussions in the new racisms of society. The discourse must help articulate how race relations are changing, becoming contradictory and are very unpredictable (Gillborn 1995a, b). Anti-racism education must also ask whether the "emphasis on cultural diversity is making invisible the politics of race" (Carby 1992: 194).

The politics of critical race studies must not provide a convenient location to engage in a politics of exclusion. This exclusionary tendency is the social reality that current ideological positions on race and anti-racism studies have to emphatically challenge, interrogate and rupture. As racial categories are reconstituted, it is clear that the social, political and intellectual meanings of race are not mutually exclusive of one another. Furthermore, the understanding of race as a specific set of social meanings does not negate the fact that racial categorization and the experience of racisms are influenced by the specificity of locations.

How racism is manifested in contemporary social relations has more to do with the construction of distance between the *self* and *other*, between *us* and *them*, in what McCarthy and Crichlow (1993) have called a politics of resentment. Omi and Winant (1994: 64) see current processes of racialization as the extension of racial meaning to previously unclassified social practices or groups. An aspect of contemporary racism (internalized racism) can be described as the reproduction of the racist discourse of the colonizer by the colonized in marginalized communities. This is clearly evident in the practice of some minority groups that critique and distance themselves from other minorities using the codes of racist language. In such situations, racial and ethnic minorities may find it difficult to form alliances that entail working collectively to fight the manifestations of dominance that continually subordinate them.

The challenge facing anti-racism is how to break away from the fixed/ rigidity of the *self/other* and *either/or* dichotomies in conventional discourses or modes of thought (see Stasiulis 1990; Suleri 1992; Brewer 1993; Grewal and Kaplan 1994). As Sullivan also notes, in critical race studies we must be able to "reject the implicit dichotomization of sameness and difference in favour of a view of the two constructs as interdependent and intersecting" (1995: 14).

Following Carby (1992: 193), then, we need to ask at what point do conceptualizations of difference feed on the rigid segregation and ghettoization of individuals and groups in society and create a "political paralysis" in the struggle for anti-racism change (Roman 1993). In fact, the struggle against White privilege is part of the struggle against ghettoization. In order to move away from the false binaryisms of race thinking, we must recognize concretely the role of White privilege in reproducing these binaryisms in the first place. "Whiteness" has powerful currency as economic property (see Harris 1993). It has a history of unquestioned access that most other races do not have. Whites need to join the struggle for anti-racism change, recognizing both their privileged positions and how they can use these positions to advance the cause of social justice and transformative change in society.

The ongoing critical study of race and anti-racism may contribute to an understanding of how, as individuals and groups, we can engage in social interactions and practices that foreground the issues of race, racism, equity and power-sharing among groups. The goal of a struggle for social change is more than to simply integrate human lives and concerns with the natural world in order to strengthen our basic humanness. It is about how we make sense of our cultural differences and recognize, affirm and engage such social differences as sites and sources of power contestation between and among groups.

Deckha (1994) has argued that, in the critical anti-racism discourse, the centrality of race is a conceptual apparatus through which to understand power differentials in society and the processes of racialized subjectivity. The notion of power used here refers to the control, production and maintenance of social values, choices and preferences. To understand power in an anti-racism discourse calls for an understanding of historical privileges. Power also takes the form of positions of material advantage and political influence.

An important learning objective of critical anti-racism is the explication of how cultural differences are produced in a racialized society organized by differential relations of power. For example, within mainstream schools minority students and their cultures are quickly constructed as deviations when these students resist assimilation into the dominant culture. Oppositional and sometimes confrontational strategies are used to this end (see Solomon 1992; Walcott 1995).

The production of race knowledge and the practice of racisms are both embedded in power relations. Dominant views in society not only articulate and justify relations of exclusion and oppression, but also tend to give a "negative evaluation" to the supposed essence of difference (Anthias and Yuval-Davis 1992: 15). How difference is named and acted upon are fundamental issues in the critical understanding of race and racist practice in society. Acknowledging and understanding difference is to question the hegemonic ideologies and dominant group norms and values that define "difference" and organize the structures within which human differences are interpreted in everyday practices of society.

The use of the race concept as an analytical and practical tool is only valid if it allows for adequate discussion and the transformation of relations of power, domination and oppression. Emphasizing the importance of the race concept in the anti-racism discourse is not meant to create a racial divide among groups. We must understand the racial divide as, in fact, caused by differentials in power. Thus, the centrality of the race concept speaks to the importance of understanding how society is racialized through historical and contemporary conditions that give rise to and sustain the production of racial boundaries.

In order to engage in thoughtful and authentic conversations and to cross any racial divide between and among groups, it is important to acknowledge the legitimacy of the varied and sometimes oppositional knowledges and shared experiences of people. This is important because in contemporary society, differential power relations are maintained and reproduced through the systemic silencing of oppositional voices that challenge dominant viewpoints and structures, and the status quo. We must avoid the suppression of individual and group identities which is an inherent feature of modern discourses on equality and sameness. These discourses are inadequate because of their failure to ground an analysis of difference in a theory of power. It is crucial, then, that emerging critical meanings of race and the understandings of the practice of multiple racisms allow for unfettered interrogation of our knowledge about difference and power within commonly shared and connected spaces. It is only in this way that we can understand what binds human groups together and be able to work collectively towards the removal of the structural and ideological barriers that divide us all along multiple points of power.

A critical anti-racism educational strategy seeks to critically contextualize the production of cultural and other forms of differences within racialized discourses (see Donald and Rattansi 1992). A new critical understanding of race and racism draws on notions of representation, difference, identity and power (McCarthy and Crichlow 1993). It questions the centrality and normativity of Whiteness, and the fact that "White" is a key concept that leads to the construction of non-Whites as "other" (see Memmi 1965; Trinh 1989, 1991; Spivak 1990; Mohanty 1990, 1991a, b; Bhabha 1994: 81). It also challenges stereotyping as a major discursive strategy (Bhabha 1994: 66) anchored in a notion of the fixity of categories. Whites, in particular, are enjoined to conduct personal examinations of their discursive processes and social practice of seeing racial minorities and so-called people of colour as "other" (see Britzman 1993; Sleeter 1994).

As already pointed out, critical anti-racism studies recognize that there is more to contend with than a simplistic Black/White duality. They refute the notion that racism is an experience that only affects the "object of its wrath" (Frankenberg 1993a). They search for an understanding of the reproduction of "Whiteness" and its masking as an unracialized category. They see "Whiteness" as "intrinsically linked to relations of domination" (ibid., 6), without necessarily falling into the trap of essentializing "White." They also hold the position that discussions of race and anti-racism do not exclude Whites because Whites are also racialized for power and privilege. Roman (1993) is clear on this issue when she states, "White is a colour!" Anti-racist Whites must first fight their own power and privilege.

A critical anti-racism approach challenges the way individuals in the dominant culture rationalize their (personal) prejudices and discriminatory actions without much personal discomfort. It questions how some members of subordinate groups internalize racist discourses, as evidenced in their relationships with other members of their own group. Consequently, it calls on subordinate group members to interrogate "how and why" they maintain social distance between themselves and the group with which they share common historical experiences of subordination and resistance. It also calls on subordinate group members to examine the extent to which they internalize the dominant group's exploitative tendencies, such that it is easy to disconnect themselves from the fight against social oppression. I am referring here, in particular, to racial minorities that accuse anti-racist activists of reinventing racism, even in its absence.

A critical anti-racism approach also seeks to develop an understanding of the nature of differential power relations through which institutionalized, racialized disenfranchisement or marginalization takes place and persists. It sees human differences as the direct consequences of unequal relationships, produced and maintained by differential power between dominant and subordinate groups. It examines contemporary processes and structures through which the most dominant in society use their positions, power, influence and techno-material advantage to appropriate the wealth and knowledge of other communities, and thereby reproduce the existing relations of domination.

Gupta and Ferguson (1992: 14), writing in another context, caution against naturalized discourses of "here" and "there," "us" and "them," "our own" and "other" societies that fail to provide a deeper understanding of human global interactions. They argue that there needs to be an explication of the "processes of production of difference in a world of culturally, socially and economically interconnected and interdependent spaces" (ibid.). For example, they assert that cultural difference is produced and maintained in a field of power relations and in a world continually differentiated through dominant discourses on immigration, nationhood and/or citizenship. It is in the maintenance of hegemonic notions of nationhood and citizenship that human differences, in particular, are negatively evaluated.

The Saliency of Skin Colour

In hegemonic social evaluations of human differences, skin colour differences have historically been used to justify unequal human treatment. Therefore, as we call for an understanding of new and alternative meanings of race, we must be careful not to deny the saliency of skin colour as this is still a key factor in the social construct of race. Race and social racism have everything to do with skin colour differences, but they involve more than skin colour. While definitions of race and racialized behaviour are historically specific and continually changing, we must be cautious of an uncritical post-modernist stance that will deny the saliency of skin colour in our lives.[4] Skin colour constitutes a basis for apportioning collective material advantage and disadvantage. In effect, skin colour is significant because it is systematically paired with material rewards and economic and political punishment (see Li and Bolaria 1988).

Admittedly, as Miles (1989, 1993) points out, there has been a tendency by some to socially construct race on the basis of skin colour alone, and thus ignore how other physical and cultural characteristics have been used as the basis of racial divisions and classifications. But to deny the social meaning of skin colour, because race is more than skin colour, is an equally problematic stance.

The negative evaluation of some forms of skin colour requires the a priori existence of an ideology of White supremacy to maximize its intended social effects. It is important to search for explanations as to why and how skin colour continues to carry a social significance in our material lives. For example, why is a specific set of physical characteristics selected as the basis for group categorization? What is the process of ascribing social, economic and political status to a racial group, based solely on skin colour? (See Spike Lee's movie, School Daze, as a problematic example of this dynamic.)

Political-economic and neo-Marxist explanations of race have pointed to the definite economic value attached to skin colour (Li and Bolaria 1988; Li 1990). Skin colour evaluation dovetails with the need for capital to exploit human labour, to appropriate group and individual resources and to distribute rewards and penalties in the contexts of scarcity and insecurity. This is understood if one recognizes that racism, like sexism and other forms of oppression, relies on political, symbolic, cultural and economic force to achieve its designed effects (see Novac 1994; cf. Millet 1985: 25).

Cox, in espousing a connection between European capitalism and naturalism, argues that until the cheap labour of Blacks was "discovered," skin colour did not carry a social significance. This explanation begs the question: "Why were

Blacks considered the 'best workers . . . for the heavy labour in the mines and plantations across the Atlantic'" (1948: 332)? Could Whites or Asians not be "best workers" as well had a racist ideology not corrupted the minds of European colonizers, merchants, plantation owners and quasi-capitalists to look elsewhere for "cheap labour?" In the critique of dominant, mainstream race knowledge, the role of ethnocentrism, in maintaining relations of domination, should not be downplayed. We cannot ignore the practical uses of the social implications of race formations, and particularly how issues of economics and patriarchy have historically helped reproduce racist, classist and sexist ideologies and dogma.

Notes

1. I am referring to ideas about Black genetic and intellectual inferiority conveyed in contemporary works of Phillip Rushton, a Canadian psychology professor at the University of Western Ontario, London, Ontario, and the book, *Bell Curve: The Reshaping of American Life by Differences of Intelligence*, authored by Richard J. Herrnstein and Charles Murray, and published by the Free Press in 1994.

2. The concept of "other" and the processes of "othering" in pre-colonial societies, whether in feudal, slave, and/or indigenous and Native communities should not be seen as synonymous with the nineteenth century's scientific conceptions of race and the processes of racializing groups for unequal material treatment. It is generally believed that the "other," as constructed in early social formations, never lost his or her basic humanity (Goldberg 1993). The creation of "cultural others" was a human appreciation of difference, and of communities and groups, rather than a means to strip individuals and groups of their basic self-decency, dignity, wealth and social knowledge. Later creations and characterizations of "others" served the material and utilitarian needs of some people (Said 1979).

3. Banking theories of education are predominantly based on assumptions that one learns in a fairly linear and direct fashion. The teacher speaks, the student listens and then uses what the teacher has said to move on to the next level or concept. The student is an empty vessel into which that teachers pour their knowledge. Issues of transmission and reception of knowledge are left largely out of the picture. This conception helps to explain age divided levels and the teacher as expert models of education. Issues of social difference and power are left entirely out of the picture. These assumptions still have considerable currency in general and among a surprising number of academics and politicians (see Curtis, Livingstone and Smaller 1992).

4. My use of post-modernism here is not in reference to its rejection of meta-narratives that "posit the primacy of one social factor in determining systemic oppressions" (Sullivan 1995: 2), nor to its relevant arguments that we are all regulated by discourse and positions of power. I am, rather, concerned by an uncritical take on post-modernism that will negate the power of common historical experiences of slave oppression and economic and political imperialism as powerful tools for organizing and understanding political action. It is important to remember that, in spite of current post-modern discourse which draws attention to our multiple, shifting and overlapping identities, skin colour has always been a powerful basis for determining the allocation of material benefits and punishments in society. It is understandable, then, that skin colour should be an important criterion around which to rally in the fight for a just redistribution of material means.

Chapter Four
The Intersections of Race, Class and Gender in the Anti-Racism Discourse

In this chapter I develop a case for why the analysis of race and racism cannot stand alone in the intellectual and political pursuit of an educational transformation which undermines social oppression. King (1994: 18) asserts the need for a new theoretical synthesis to rewrite knowledge in the academy. This is in part because of the incapacity of existing theory to provide a more complete account of human and social development. Legitimate concerns are being raised, particularly by marginalized and minority groups in society, about how conventional discourses do not adequately inform knowledge producers and consumers about the totality of human experiences. We need to reject "essences/ totalizing discourses," (King 1994) and work to articulate comprehensive forms of knowledge that reveal an understanding of how our multiple identities and subject positions affect our very existence. Russo (1991: 303) quotes Evelyn Glenn in a poignant remark that our individualities, "histories and experiences are not just diverse, they are intertwined and interdependent."

I am introducing the notion of *integrative anti-racism studies* to address the problem of discussing the social constructs of race, class, gender and sexuality as exclusive and independent categories. Elsewhere (Dei 1994b), I have defined integrative anti-racism as the study of how the dynamics of social difference (race, class, gender, sexual orientation, physical ability, language and religion) are mediated in people's daily experiences. Integrative anti-racism is also an activist theory and analysis that must always be consciously linked to struggles against oppression. Integrative anti-racism acknowledges our multiple, shifting and often contradictory identities and subject positions. Borrowing from post-modernism, integrative anti-racism rejects meta-narratives or grand theories. Integrative anti-racism, in effect, calls for multiplicative, rather than additive, analyses of social oppression. It is conceded that an additive analysis denies the complexity of experiences that can, and must, be examined, explained and addressed.

Integrative anti-racism provides an understanding of how different forms of social oppression and privilege have been historically constituted. It identifies how forms of social marginality and structured dominance intersect and shift with changing conditions in society. Since one of the key objectives of the transformative project of anti-racism is to critique and deal with human injustice, all the different forms of oppression, defined along racial, ethnic, class and sexual lines, must be problematized. We cannot hope to transform society by removing only one form of oppression. There is a common link between all oppressions in the material production of society; all forms of oppression establish material and symbolic advantages for the oppressor. Any resistance to bringing the diverse and varied forms of social oppression into the anti-racism debate should be exposed both for its myopic focus and its capacity to politically paralyze social movement building. It is also destructive to fight against one form of oppression while using patterns of another to do so. An example would be a White male adult using the strap on a White child to teach the child not to be racist against a Black child. This tactic may punish racist behaviour, but it leaves physical violence as a method of controlling others and adult authority over children solidly in place.

An understanding of how race, class, gender and sexuality are interconnected in our lives will work against the construction of hierarchies of social oppression. Such hierarchies can take the form of a naive relativism and divide and fragment a movement. Racism, sexism, heterosexism and classism function in myriad forms. Integrative anti-racism therefore seeks a non-hierarchical discussion of social oppressions without assuming that all forms of oppression are unified, consistent and necessarily equal in their social effects (see Burbules and Rice 1991). This understanding follows from a recognition of the theoretical inadequacy of singular, exclusive constructs when it comes to explaining the diversity of human experiences of oppression. There is also an awareness of the need to reject "dichotomous logic . . . [that] oversimplifies and limits the scope of analysis" (Sullivan 1995: 3; see also Stasiulis 1990; Brewer 1993; Grewal and Kaplan 1994). These critiques arise out of an analytical context in which the complexity of peoples' historical and daily experiences are continuously distorted. For example, too often intellectual discourses conflate race with black(ness) and gender with women (Carby 1982a). At times too, the "conflation of race and class has been found to engender anti-Semitism by obscuring the range of class positions occupied by Jews in North America" (Sullivan 1995: 4; cf. Nestel 1993: 71).

Brewer (1993: 16) critiques dichotomous/binary oppositional modes of thought which employ *either/or* categorizations rather than *both/and* perspectives when theorizing the simultaneity, embeddedness and connectedness of myriad oppressions. An integrative anti-racism approach is based on the principle that myriad forms of oppressions are interlocked and that a study of one such system, racism, necessarily entails a study of class, gender, sexual inequalities, homophobia and ableism (see Mercer and Julien 1988). The complex nature of oppressions, and the interchangeability of the roles of "oppressor" and "oppressed" in different situations, necessitate the use of an integrative anti-racism approach to understanding social oppression. This approach is informed by the knowledge that individual subjectivities are constituted differently by the relations of race, class, gender, age, disability, sexuality, nationality, religion, language and culture.

The following discussion of integrative anti-racism primarily (but not exclusively) focuses on the three basic categories/constructs of race, class and gender. Belkhir and Ball make the interesting argument that, while "religion, sexual or political preference, [and] physical ability" are important issues affecting the human experience and condition, they "are often the result of the primary ascribed statuses" of race, class and gender. They add that the complex mixture of these social constructs "above all else influences our socialization, emotions, thought process, ideology, self-concept and our social identity." The authors further point out that "issues like religion, sexual or political preference and physical ability may certainly be examined more thoroughly through the interactive and triadic relation of race, [gender] and class" (1993: 4). But I would argue that sexual orientation, ability and religion can play primary roles in a person's lived experiences, particularly given the prevalence of heterosexism, homophobia and anti-Semitism which are particularly significant in, but not exclusive to, Euro-Western influenced societies (see also Fanon 1967).

The study of integrative anti-racism raises some important questions about social inequality: How are class divisions maintained and produced in the face of emerging and complex social identities? What qualifies as "difference" among the factors which shape and define human relations in racialized, classed and gendered contexts? How will a conception of interlocking systems of oppression, that reinforce each other and have multiple effects on individuals, avoid points of conflict? How can we prevent differences from becoming sites of competition for the primacy of one subordination or oppression over another? How do we challenge discursively imposed social identities? Perhaps most of these questions will only be answered in the actual process of doing educational and political work.

In order to respond effectively to some of these questions it is important that we view integrative anti-racism as a critical study of the social and material relations of the production of social oppressions. We must understand the material conditions for the persistence and reproduction of racism, sexism, classism, homophobia, ableism and other forms of social oppression. The political and academic goal of integrative anti-racism is to address all oppressive relations constructed along lines of difference. An integrative approach to understanding social oppressions must thus examine closely the *politics of difference*, recognizing the materiality of human existence, that is, the material consequences of myriad social identities and subjectivities. The roots of social oppression lie in material conditions and the access to property, privilege and power (see Joyce 1995b; Ng, Stanton and Scane 1995). All social relations are firmly embedded in material relations. All social relations have material consequences. The politics of integrative anti-racism arise from the collective position of material disadvantage that many people find themselves locked into, and the desire to work for a just redistribution of material means.

Notwithstanding the possible tensions between bland talk about diversity and the real question of power asymmetries around the notion of difference, it is important that the social categories of race, class, gender and sexuality are not seen as competing for primacy. There is a natural contestation that must be accepted and struggled with and against if the fight against oppression is to be successful. The study of race, class, gender and sexuality in critical anti-racism work should be pursued as an integrated approach to understanding the lived (social and material) realities of people. A foregrounding of race in the integrative anti-racism approach should not mean the exclusion of class, gender and sexual orientation. Integrative anti-racism has to address the intersectionality of class, gender and sexual orientation (sexuality). Classism, sexism and homophobia do not disappear because race has become the central focus. The lived experience of those who face racism daily from others is one where they must also face inter/ intra-racial classism, sexism and homophobia. I have more to say about this later in this chapter.

How do the complex politics of social difference articulate with material-economic interests? Rizvi (1995) rightly calls on educators to avoid a celebratory approach to social difference which may only serve the hegemonic interests of industrial capital. For example, the state's approach to multiculturalism adopts a superficial definition and treatment of culture, as reflected in the celebratory practices of the "saris, samosas and steel-bands syndrome" (Donald and Rattansi 1992: 2). Events like international cultural days can constitute opportune times for big business to make huge profits without any fundamental challenge to power relations in society. For example, the initial movement to bring multiculturalism into the classroom did not address the lived experiences of peoples of colour; rather, such a move focused on the more simplistic "getting to know you" move of consuming and observing "ethnic foods", dancing and dress. As we examine how difference is perceived in society, Rizvi (1995) suggests certain fundamental questions should be asked. For example, why the focus on difference? In whose interests is difference being presented and for what material purposes and consequences? We might also ask about the timing and sequencing of the uses and constructions of social difference. What qualifies as difference? No doubt there are some powerful academic and political forces more than ready to co-opt the language of difference and diversity to serve their own material needs and concerns.

bell hooks cautions against constructing a politics of difference in the academy to serve the intellectual interests of an emerging post-modern discourse. She argues that post-modern theory should not simply appropriate the experience of otherness to enhance the intellectual discourse of post-modernity. Post-modern theory should not separate the "politics of difference from the politics of racism" (hooks 1990: 26). Integrative anti-racism must be critical of how current articulations of multiple identities are/can be manipulated in the space of dominant, hegemonic discourses, particularly in academia (see Carty 1991a; Bannerji 1991a; Fumia 1995: 9).

An integrative approach to anti-racism must examine conventional understandings of the politics of identity. Hall offers one such critique when he references Marxian theory on identity; he talks about the fact that there are always "conditions to identity which the subject cannot construct" (1979: 16; see also Hall 1991). Bhabha also writes about the fact that "the visibility of the racial/cultural 'other' is at once a point of identity" (1994: 81). Hall and Bhabha make different but connected points. On the one hand, identity construction is a point of power and, therefore, difference. To claim difference is to have the power to claim one's difference as identity. On the other hand, as Hall points out, one is never entirely in control of the mechanisms of identity construction, like language, for example. However, one is not entirely controlled by the identity construction of others either. Bhabha is suggesting that the identification of others is also the moment of self-identification. Identities are not static, we are forever negotiating who and what we are. Social identities are constructed beyond notions of race, class, gender, sexuality, language and culture to the actual practices engaged in by people in the course of daily social interactions. It is crucial to a progressive politics of identity to understand that identity is not entirely dependent on categories of difference because social practice transgresses these boundaries all the time. We are not entirely constrained by the categories of race, class and gender. They are coercive and resilient structures in our lives, but they do not define the limits of social action. Our identities, then, are made in social interaction in concert with and using categories of difference and identity. In order to effectively organize for political change, we first have to recognize and understand that identity is defined by who the individual is, how the individual self is understood in relation to others, and how such constructions of social identities match or do not match what people actually do in their daily lives.

Of equal importance, a politics of identity involves politicizing identity. It moves beyond the mere recognition and acknowledgement of identities to engage in effective political action. Identity must provide the basis for political struggle, but as others have pointed out, identity itself is not political action (Bourne 1987: 22; Train 1995). The conventional "identity politics" prioritized an essentialized, ahistorical and nonmaterialist identity (Fuss 1989). Train (1995) argues that "identity politics" eliminated the political by focusing too much on the personal. It is important for a distinction to be made between "who am I?" and "what is to be done" (Bourne 1987: 1)? These two questions are connected. One needs to know the self in order to engage in political action. But

Anti-Racism Education

change cannot happen simply from knowing oneself. We have to find answers to the questions, "what is to be done and how?"

Thus, in a sense, the importance of adopting an integrative approach to anti-racism studies is captured in the intersections between issues of identity and social practices. The study of the concept of race is a study of representation as defined by identity, identification and social practices. Racism, as a set of material practices, is about unequal power relations. It is also about how people relate to each other on the basis of defined social identities and identifications. These reasonings implicate how we organize politically for change; they move us beyond questions about *who we are* to discussions about *what we do*. We must search for connections between identity and social practices (see Britzman 1993). Our everyday local social networks are increasingly structuring and governing our daily experiences.

Below I will explore this topic further in the context of six interrelated key issues underlying integrative anti-racism studies. The *first* is an understanding of the *process of articulation* of social difference. Integrative anti-racism speaks to the need to examine the social categories of difference in order to understand their points of "articulation" and connection with each other. The articulations of race, class, gender and sexuality produce sites of complex human social differences, rather than sites and sources of a celebratory approach to diversity. They are "rupturing these social categories"; thus, we need to recognize, understand and engage our multiple subject positions and to work for alternative futures. Feminist writers such as Carby (1982a), Mohanty (1990), Collins (1990), hooks (1990), Carty, (1991a, b), Bannerji (1991a, b) and Mullings (1992), among many others, have articulated varying ideas about multiple subjectivities to illustrate the intersections of oppressions in the everyday experiences of so-called women of colour. Many, if not all, of these authors speak from their embodied selves while making the connections between their individual and collective identities and their own experiences.

Integrative anti-racism is a critical analysis of how current understandings of the dynamics of social difference relate to issues of identity and subjectivity. It moves away from establishing a hierarchy of difference and an exclusive and problematic concern with the "other." Integrative anti-racism does not see the *self* as that which *other* is not. Human experiences are dialectically shaped by questions of social difference, by history and by socio-political contexts. The existence of multiple identities has some significance for how individuals live their lives and relate to each other in society, and how individuals come to understand society and work collectively for change.

Belkhir and Ball (1993), in their interesting discussion of the dynamics of social difference, point out the complex mixture of race, class and gender, and how these categories influence everything we do as humans. Our social world is structured by power relations of race, ethnicity, class, gender and sexuality (see also Collins 1993; Roscigno 1994). Individuals do not simply and solely fit into one specified category as an oppressor or the oppressed. One can be oppressed and an oppressor at the same time and at different times.

For example, as an anti-racist educator, I must acknowledge my own privileged middle-class background when speaking to students about "oppression." There is the question of the relational aspect of oppression (Freire 1990), there is the "nonsynchrony of oppression" (McCarthy 1988), and there is the problematic of a discourse of "humanization as a universal without considering the various definitions this term may [acquire]" from individuals of different positionalities and from diverse social groups (Weiler 1991: 453). I have to be aware of how my views as I present them in the classroom, by way of instruction or through interaction with students, could be maintaining social privilege and power. My power as a Black, middle-class, heterosexual male teacher may often work to make me forget that, while I am debating and struggling against race oppression, I might be marginalizing women and other peoples oppressed by reason of, for example, their class or sexuality. Such understandings are fundamental to any attempt to theorize the connections between social differences and oppression in the integrative anti-racism discourse.

Each individual goes through a variety of experiences in a lifetime and theoretical articulations of social reality have to reflect the intersections of such various experiences. For example, when a Southeast Asian male executive living in Canada loses his job and eventually goes on welfare, his lifetime experiences, relating to all his subject positions, come into play. We cannot essentialize race, class and gender categories. These are socially constructed categories whose social meanings and actualities in the daily experiences of peoples not only overlap but also shift in time and space. We need to understand the systemic and structural character of these social categories and how they function as social ideologies (see King 1994: 10).

Fumia brings an interesting perspective to discussions of articulations of identities and political action, stressing the importance of knowing our multiple subject positions and the frustrations associated with this practice. In identifying herself as a "middle-class white female," she talks about her frustrations with the term. She asks: "How do those words locate anyone? Middle-class white female conflates differences in economics, subjectivities and colours. Yet, because my life intersects with enough of the stereotypical aspects of the category, how do I position myself elsewhere" (1995: 9)? For me, Fumia's question is important as it draws attention to the difficulty of placing individuals into neatly conceptualized boxes that will allegedly capture the complexity of their identities and experiences. If this is a difficult project for individuals, how can we then engage in academic discussions as if everything about our world is so neatly packaged and stationary?

It is thus important for an integrative approach to social oppression to disaggregate social categories such as race, class, gender and sexuality along multiple dimensions to see, for example, how race articulates with other forms of oppression. Joyce (1995b: 7) posits that, as a White person, she has unearned privileges and material advantages because of the physical characteristics that Euro-Canadian/American society deems as "racially white and of highest value." But she argues that the material consequences of being a woman is the absence of power and a lack of resources that one collectively shares with other women. Women, she points out, experience a "relative position of structurally and materially less power and privilege" than men in a particularly sexist, patriarchal society (ibid.: 4). However, to be a woman of racial minority background is to have even relatively less material power and privilege in a patriarchal, White-dominated society. But even among women of racial minority backgrounds, class differences can be apparent. For example, there are differences in terms of those occupying relative positions of wealth and influence (e.g., a bank executive or university professor) and those who are employed in jobs with lower status and are paid barely enough to support the household they head.

The significance of adopting an integrative perspective of anti-racism is illustrated by the unique oppressions that Black working-class women, for example, experience in Euro-Canadian/American societies. Black feminist scholars (hooks 1988; King 1988; Collins 1990; Dill and Zinn 1990; Carty 1991a, b; Zinn 1991) have argued that the unique oppression experienced by Black women has to be understood in the context of how the dialectical relationships of race, class and gender are played out in women's daily lives. The social construction of a Black, working-class mother's position in North American society has been one of the ways for mainstream society to maintain hegemony over production relations within the White hetero-patriarchal, capitalist system (Carty 1991a, 20; Ng 1993a, b). Black, working-class women have historically and contemporarily been constructed as a source of labour for the state. The historical role and position of Black "immigrant" nurses in the reproduction of economic wealth for the Canadian state is a well-documented example that race cannot be understood outside of gender and class constructions (Calliste 1991, 1993a, 1993b, 1994a).

As Zinn (1991: 6) has shown, it is not simply that gender cannot be understood outside of race and class. Gender is experienced differently within each racial framework and class group. Subordinate racial groups of all classes are subject to racial oppression and, while members of dominant racial groups may be oppressed by means of gender oppression, their membership in a racial group is not a source of oppression. Furthermore, class and gender differences in society are complicated by the harsh realities of intra-group oppression among members of the same socially constructed racial framework.[1] The exploitative working conditions of many "immigrant women" working in the homes of middle-class families in Canada are a well-documented case (see Ng and Ramirez 1981; Ng 1988). The task of integrative anti-racism is to unravel these interlocking systems of oppression in order to be able to intellectually articulate and engage in meaningful and progressive political action to address social injustice and oppression.

The *second* and related issue of interest in integrative anti-racism studies is the relevance of *personal experiential knowledge* and the specific ways our multiple subject positions and identities affect our ways of creating knowledge. Knowledge is produced out of a series of socio-political arrangements, such as the particular intersections of social oppressions. Lived, personal experience is central to the formulation of any social knowledge. Matsuda (1989) discusses the importance and relevance of seeing the world as experienced by the oppressed if we are to achieve effective political action and change. However, as Burbules and Rice (1991: 405) caution, we must guard against an over-valorization of personal experiential knowledge in which "external" forces mediating and/or impinging upon such knowledge are considered "coercive and imperialistic." We must also resist the temptation of presenting ourselves as not-to-be-questioned voices of authority merely because we are speaking from experience.

Sullivan points out that an integrative theory of anti-racism "draws on the actual lived experiences of individuals as a basis for intellectual inquiry" (1995: 5) and engagement in politics of change. The work of feminist scholars Weiler (1991: 469), Russo (1991: 300) and Collins (1990: 207–09) shows that the personal experiences and a self-reflective critique of the experiential reality are important bases from which to pursue integrative anti-racism work. Weiler speaks about the different kinds of knowledge that can be uncovered when women question their daily experiences and their collective experiences with regard to the interlocking systems of oppression. She makes reference to the everyday experiences of so-called women of colour and of lesbian women "whose very being challenges existing racial, sexual, heterosexual and class dominance [and] . . . leads to a knowledge of the world that both acknowledges differences, and points to the need for an integrated analysis and practice" in relation to the interlocking systems of oppression (Weiler 1991: 468: cf. Combahee River Collective 1981: 3, 275).

Collins (1990) and Russo (1991) also argue that experience and practice are the contextual bases of integrative anti-racism knowledge; they link this practice and experience to theory. Both authors call for a self-reflective critique and validation of personal experiences of the relational aspects of difference as part of the process of creating theoretical and practical knowledge for social transformation. Individuals must be able to articulate and critically reflect upon their own experiences and their accumulated personal knowledge about the workings of the inner self and questions of identity, in order to work collectively for change (see also hooks 1993, 1994).

The *third* issue concerns developing an understanding of how *differential power and privilege* work in society. The study of the dynamics of social difference is also a study of differential power relations. Power relations are embedded in social relations of difference. Thus, an understanding of the intersections of difference is more than a preparedness to hear each other out. It involves more than providing the means and opportunities for subordinated groups to empower themselves and find creative solutions to their own concerns. It is about ensuring that all social groups have decision-making power; safety provisions and equitable access to, and control over, the valued goods and services of society with which to attain human dignity and individual and collective survival.

Therefore, an integrative approach to anti-racism studies explores the use of power to differentiate, discriminate and establish material advantage and disadvantage among and between peoples and groups. Social power and economic advantage are intertwined. Understanding the relational aspects of social difference means delving into the critique of micro and macro structures of power and how these structures mediate peoples' daily experiences. It draws attention to the larger socio-political contexts in which the fragmented categories of race, class, gender and sexuality intersect in daily social practices. Attention is paid to the material needs of individuals and groups in society and how these needs are sanctioned and stratified through social relations of domination and subordination. For example, it is about understanding how the hegemony of the market economy affects the schooling experiences of minority youth. How this is manifested in schools can be attested to in the differential positions that students occupy according to their race, ethnicity, class, gender and sexual orientation. Many studies demonstrate a clearly disproportionate representation of African-Canadian/American students from working-class backgrounds in vocational courses rather than in the "academic" courses which lead students into universities (Oakes 1985; Brown 1993; see also Fine 1991).

Integrative anti-racism examines the power of subordinated groups to resist positions of marginality through individual agency and collective will. It interrogates how groups positioned differently in society can nevertheless come together on the basis of a common abhorrence of social oppression and fight the prevailing culture of dominance. While recognizing the power of human agency, an integrative anti-racism approach also locates significant responsibility for change in the arena of those who control the structural means to effecting fundamental change in society, that is, those who control the apparatus of the state. This is an example of where the intersections of social class become important. Social power is generally in the hands of the ruling class which comprises mostly White heterosexual males. It is thus difficult to speak about power and not highlight class. The bourgeoisie will not give up power easily since it will not be in their interest to do so. This means it will take the collective effort of the relatively powerless groups to work and bring this change about.

The *fourth* issue of concern relates to the *saliency of race* in an integrative anti-racism discourse. In recognizing the centrality of race and its "immediacy in everyday experience" (Omi and Winant 1994), integrative anti-racism also acknowledges the co-determinant status of race, class and gender dynamics. Integrative anti-racism is based on the understanding that race relations in society are actually interactions between raced, classed and gendered subjects. Thus, in theorizing integrative anti-racism, race becomes the main point of entry through which the varied forms of social oppression can and must be understood.

While it is true that we live in a society structured by relations of race, ethnicity, class, gender, sexuality and ability, among others, we nevertheless make political choices every moment and every day of our lives. Giving saliency and centrality to race and racial oppression in a critical anti-racism educational practice should not be seen as an attempt to hierarchize and/or privilege one form of social oppression over another. It is *a political decision*. Admittedly, selecting one form of human experience as a point of entry may render another experience invisible. Yet, we cannot adequately simultaneously explore all experiences with the same vigour and intensity. Therefore, we should attempt to capture, as much as possible, from the points where they intersect with one particular form of social oppression the diversity and multiplicity of human experiences. Racism should neither be subsumed nor separated from all forms of oppression. Bannerji's (1993) work is exemplary in this regard when she discusses racist sexism and sexist racism. The fight for equity should not be seen as a zero sum game that pits Blacks against Whites, women against men, heterosexuals against homosexuals, Christians against non-Christians, Canadian immigrants against First Nations peoples.

But, as we recognize the matrix of domination and subordination and conceptualize racism, sexism and classism as interactive, interlocking and mutually reinforcing systems of oppression, we must also validate the saliency and visibility of certain forms of oppression (see Collins 1993). For how can we understand and transform social reality without recognizing or acknowledging that certain forms/systems of domination and oppression are more salient and visible than others for different groups in different contexts? How do we explain the situational and contextual variations and intensities of different forms of oppression? For example, how do we account for the fact that a single, Black middle-class woman is kept out of a White neighbourhood when trying to rent or buy a house, because of her race and gender? Are we not trivializing social oppression by claiming that we are all oppressors and oppressed?

The answer to this last question is complex and deserves further comment. As Bunch (1987: 88–9) has pointed out, when individuals identify themselves according to their victimization as a member of an oppressed group, there is less ability for them to see their own agency and power to effect change. Others may also begin to identify themselves as "victims of oppression" and fail to see the severity of other forms of oppression because they are so narrowly focused on their own victimization. This is problematic, particularly when that form of oppression may not have a material basis but is experienced more as a hurtful, restrictive practice. For example, Black students can use discriminatory words or engage in discriminatory actions (such as telling White students that they cannot join in a basketball game because they cannot slam-dunk) which may not have material consequences for White students. My point is that Black racism does not deny material wealth to Whites.

Nevertheless, the concept of oppression may be helpful for those who are highly privileged in society and are just beginning to learn what social oppression really is. It helps these individuals to place their own grounded experiences of oppression, no matter how comparatively trivial in relation to more widespread and sustained forms of oppression that marginalized groups regularly experience, in a webbed system of domination/subjugation. To find one's place in the web, these individuals must begin to see the whole web and how various oppressions are played off each other horizontally to keep the systems of oppression in place. It is thus a useful beginning to allow each individual to talk about his or her own oppressions. It provides an opportunity to make that first crucial step which is to enter into the discussion about oppression. Issues about the location of multiple identities, and analysis of the implications, intersections and variable degrees of material consequences of different oppressions can be pursued once the concept of oppression is connected to one's personal experience and that experience is located in the total web of systemic oppressions.

Historically, in movements for social change, race concerns have always been pushed to the background or denied. So the decision to recognize the saliency and centrality of race is, in part, taken to ensure that race as an issue in the struggle for change is not lost. Similarly, in a hetero-patriarchal capitalist society, gender, sexuality and class issues are conveniently denied. But there have been, and continue to be, insidious attempts to misplace race and racism from social critique and political agenda for change. An example of this is the constant questioning of "what does race mean?" or the declaration that "racism does not exist" or "we are all one race." Integrative anti-racism will thus have to contend with the ways that all of us are burdened with this history of racism as a social, material and political practice, as well as the ways we come to know, understand and interpret racism. Racism and its varied manifestations have to be front and centre in the anti-racism discourse.

Are there different articulations of racisms within social class, sexuality and gender categories (see Anthias and Yuval-Davis 1992: 15)? In coming to understand the dynamics of social difference, individuals can and will articulate similar ideas differently given their social realities. This requires that, to avoid negating or denying certain aspects of our experiences, we are able to discuss these experiences, showing their intersections with our multiple subjectivities.

A conceptual and analytical distinction must be made between anti-oppression and anti-racism studies. While there are broad similarities and points of connection between *"integrative anti-racism"* and *"anti-oppression"* studies, there are important distinctions between the two. The integrative anti-racism approach sees race as both the first point of entry and a point which does not lose its position of centrality during subsequent analyses of intersecting oppression. Joyce argues that "anti-oppression education does not presume a single central point of entry nor a central point of analysis . . . it presumes multiple positions of identity by which an individual enters the discourse on social oppression [and] . . . . some of those identities are individually experienced as central, and some are marginal" (1995b: 6). As individuals, we possess diverse identities that variously describe who and what we are, and what we politically and consciously choose as our points of entry into discussions about oppression. In anti-oppression studies, race is one of many entry points. But it is important we also recognize that "some forms of oppression have a particularly substantial material base" when compared to others (ibid.: 6). For example, the impact of institutionalized racism on the job opportunities and wages of marginalized racial groups has a material impact that is different from the impact of racist language. In deciding on our entry points, we must make explicit our subject locations and the relative power, privileges and disadvantages, as well as the experiential knowledge and the political assumptions that we bring to the discussion. What is important in this discussion is the convergence and alliance between integrative anti-racism and anti-oppression studies. We must speak of and act on the alliances in these struggles if successful change is to happen.

Social oppression is a topic that elicits pain, anger, shame, guilt, fear and uneasiness in people. People are likely to engage the subject from diverse vantage points. For me, the experience of racism, while not diminishing its connections with other forms of oppression, runs deep. I know more about racism, perhaps, than I do about other forms of oppression, not simply because I have chosen to take the time to learn about racism, but more so because it has been a very significant part of my experience, particularly in North America (see also hooks 1984: 11). There is a prior personal and collective history that cannot be ignored. We have to deal with the historical fact that, in past academic discussions about myriad oppressions and other "isms," the topic of racism has often been pushed to the background or omitted altogether. This is what informs Enid Lee when she strongly recommends that we put "racism at the foreground, and then include the others by example and analysis" (*Rethinking Schools* 1991: 3) to illustrate the powerful connections to other forms of oppression.

The foregoing discussion also indicates that while educators stress integrative and relational aspects of difference (race, class, gender and sexuality), they must be critical of post-modern discourse that will deny the saliency of racial oppression in the anti-racism political project. Racism is what most educators and many other people are either afraid to talk about or continually and conveniently choose to ignore. While the integrative anti-racism strategy is to ensure that race is not given an exclusive pre-eminence, it must also avoid a "political paralysis" (Roman 1993) in the struggle for change. As educators, we can make pragmatic choices as to how to take up and centre race analysis for political education and for educational advocacy. It should also be possible for educators and members of society to engage in a theoretical discussion of race issues that speak foremost and most appropriately to social reality and economic materiality.

The *fifth* concern involves extending discussions about integrative anti-racism to include *global political economic* issues. Central to this is building an understanding of how current processes of globalization relate to questions of identity and social practice in Euro-Canadian/American contexts. My objective is not to re-engage in any detail the classical debates about whether or not race, gender and sexuality can be understood in terms of the analytical approach of historical materialism, or whether race, gender and sexuality must be accorded an analytical status separate and distinct from class (Marx 1853; Simmel 1950; Gabriel and Ben-Tovim 1979; see also Miles 1980). I am more interested in showing how global political economy issues (Stasiulis 1990; Satzewich 1990) relate to the integrative anti-racism dialogue and the political struggle for social change. As the discussion in Chapter Three shows, a biological-genetic explanation of race (and gender) emerged prior to the institutionalization of capitalism and slavery. This fact neither denies the centrality of slavery in the development of capitalism, nor the significant role of capitalism in institutionalizing racism (see Cox 1948, 1976; Williams 1964).

Neo-Marxist analysis of society may inform the progressive politics of integrative anti-racism change. All current forms of social oppressions are the products of a system of capitalist insurgence and domination. In fact, many scholars have pointed to the need for the critical analysis of race, class and gender intersections to be placed in the context of global capitalism (see, for example, Bannerji 1991a; Carty 1993; Ng 1993a, b). Local problems of race, class and gender relations have their global dimensions. It is for these reasons that a narrow conception of integrative anti-racism politics must be rejected. Ongoing processes of restructuring capital at global, regional and national levels are having a deleterious impact on the ability of many individuals and groups to meet basic economic and material needs. A consequence of modern capital flows and exchanges, particularly the globalization of capital, is the growing feminization of poverty and the racialization of working-class politics. Working-class politics is now "race sensitive." Much work is curently being done to address racism within working-class groups, and some ruling groups are using race and racism as a way to divide working-class movements. There are mounting antagonisms and competitions between and among groups, communities and nations over access to, and control over, drastically maldistributed economic and productive resources.

Undoubtedly, globalization, defined as a process of increased social, political and economic international integration, driven primarily (but not exclusively) by the interests and dictates of modern industrial and transnational capital, has produced some challenges that need to be addressed by anti-racism education. Globalization is the new justification used by Euro-Canadian/American society for asserting its political and economic dominance over indigenous and colonized peoples. Globalization has resulted in a crisis of knowledge about human society, a crisis manifested in the contradictions and tensions of a competitive knowledge economy, the internationalization of labour and the concomitant struggles over power-sharing among social groups. Globalization has also accelerated the flow of cultures across geographical, political and cultural borders. Cultural borders can be marked by a language or concentrations of one racial or ethnic group within a diverse population, or by more malleable cultural forms like dress and music. Cultural borders are not necessarily materially or geographically constrained. Any agenda for educational and social transformation must be able to deal with the dilemmas and contradictions inherent in the trend towards cultural homogenization, cultural differentiation and cultural revitalization in our societies.[2]

These are far-reaching concerns because the knowledge crisis is not restricted to the so-called metropolitan centres of the world. Within local communities, as Zarate (1994) points out, the crisis of knowledge can be seen in the fragmentation of traditional values and beliefs, the erosion of spirituality and the distortions in local, regional and national economies. The commodification of knowledge and culture across space and time also has implications which reach far beyond jeopardizing the integrity of local cultural production. For example, the so-called developing world continues to vigorously confront current insidious attempts at cultural, economic and political recolonization which take the form of educational reforms driven by the interests of corporate, transnational capital. The workers in the Chiapas resistance against the Mexican government and the North American Free Trade Agreement (NAFTA) is an example of a developing nation confronting the invasion of capitalist practice and ideology. This example is particularly significant in that the resistance comes from subordinated groups in Mexico and demonstrates the similarity of interests among the ruling classes of different countries.

The harsh economic lessons of globalization clearly point to the urgent need for a new approach to education that responds appropriately to the challenge of difference and diversity in communities internationally. In Euro-Canadian/American circles, current academic and political projects of rupturing hegemonic social science paradigms have added fuel to the demand of marginalized communities for education to respond to the pressing concerns of racism, sexism, classism and other forms of oppressive and discriminatory practices that diminish our basic humanity. In fact, anti-racism education emerged as a consequence of the ongoing transformations in social science epistemologies to offer alternative readings of how, as social beings, we live our lives in multi-racial, multi-ethnic, pluralistic communities.

Each individual in society lives and experiences different material realities. Nevertheless, we are all governed by a set of socio-political and structural conditionalities. There must be some awareness on the part of anti-racism educators and practitioners of the structures, constraints, limitations and possibilities embedded in the wider social contexts. This awareness is fundamental to political work for an alternative society (see Brewer 1993: 15). For example, the practice of integrative anti-racism education needs to recognize at all levels the forces of political rigidity and economic constraints that obstruct the envisioning and actualization of alternative social formations.

There are substantial socio-economic and demographic changes taking place internationally, nationally and locally that have significant consequences for human interactions and relations. Codjoe lists some of the changes as "a general shift in the national (economies) from goods-producing to service-intensive industries; an increasing bifurcation of the labour market into low-wage/high-wage sectors; technological innovation; the relocation out and/or de-industrialization of the manufacturing sectors of major cities; and a re-constitution of the social composition of the work force which now consists mainly of women and minorities" (1995: 2). These developments have implications for social relations defined along lines of difference. Particularly, the economic recession in North America and most of Europe in the 1980s provided the "scene for the re-emergence of race as a salient issue in political and public debates" (ibid.) when unemployment and poverty forced people to look for scapegoats for the economic hardships. One look at the policies of the Mike Harris-lead Ontario government of the mid 1990s shows how those in power can use seemingly neutral economic problems to attack the rights of marginalized groups.

Economic depression has heightened an awareness of "otherness" among some members of White Canadian society, making racial minorities the focus of people's anger. The transition from industry-based economies to high technology economies continues to create economic turmoil due to high unemployment rates and poverty. Class differences have been accentuated and the working class are fearful of what the future holds. Classism is gaining currency just as much as racism, sexism, homophobia and xenophobia.

The current ultra-conservative rhetoric, utilizing racist code words to blame racial minorities and women for the most recent economic problems, has an appeal to many lower middle- and working-class Whites (particularly males) in Euro-Canadian/American society. But there are clear examples in the apportioning of blame of the intersections of class, race and gender. Many White women do not accept the blame, just as some Black men may accept the rhetoric blaming women for some societal problems. This is because of the prevailing economic climate of diminishing wages, increasing unemployment and economic insecurity (see Apple 1993). In particular, dominant group members of middle-class backgrounds see their privileges under assault and their class positions weakening in the face of globalization and the downward trends in national economies. This may, in part, explain the election of the Progressive Conservatives in the 1995 Ontario provincial election as they basically promised to punish the poor and protect the "beleaguered middle-class" in their election campaign.

Within the Canadian context, many people, irrespective of class, racial and gender backgrounds, are threatened by national and international economic insecurity. Whites, particularly men, have more to lose since economic disparities rely upon racist and patriarchal power structures which provide unequal access to opportunities and resources. In a context of political and economic insecurity, those with the highest vested interest in maintaining material advantage are the most likely to feel threatened by further destabilizing forces that question their advantage. They speak up to protect the status quo.

In the Euro-Canadian/American context this is made apparent by voices of criticism over such issues as employment equity and affirmative action policies. Agents of oppression become very defensive about being exposed and will use whatever (considerable) means in their power and influence to bury, hide and deflect their agency. Examples of such strategies appear in the "take the offensive," blame someone or scapegoat the poor, Blacks, women and feminism's attitude in order to avoid responsibility for agency as part of the "oppressor" group. Others deny the inequality or divest themselves from membership in the oppressing group and instead focus on individual agency. Other strategies include shifting the frame of reference of debate completely to nullify or stymie the argument so as to maintain control of the agenda. Sometimes too, those who wield power and have the means to do so will attempt to silence opponents or critics or even have someone else speak on their "behalf." Others will plead the cause of "fairness" or "reasonableness" in order to fall back into normalcy and the familiarity of existing conditions. My argument is that, rather than question the Canadian government's economic policies and the activities of private and corporate organizations, some Canadians, especially those feeling most threatened, decide to vent their anger on "immigrants," racial minorities, the working poor, those who are not employed and women.

Therefore, discussions of racism and public discourses which blame marginal and disempowered groups for economic problems must recognize institutionalized poverty through bringing class issues seriously into the anti-racism debate (see Troyna 1993: 11). Integrative anti-racism cannot sufficiently deal with the problem of racial oppression without simultaneously confronting the structural problems of economic poverty, cultural sexism,[3] and capitalist patriarchy. Integrative anti-racism must interrogate how current social formations continue to reproduce conditions of abject poverty in the midst of affluence and plenty for a few. In doing so, it must guard against reductionistic arguments that pit class against race. Such arguments fit well with the ideological position that class inequality is the fundamental problem of human social relations. And the neo-conservatives would argue that, through paid labour and hard work, people can overcome racial subordination. But, class relations are not only sustained by material (economic) relations. Class is also a social identity constructed through ideological and symbolic practices.

Race, class, gender and sexuality mutually affect each other. An integrative anti-racism approach must reject analyses which reduce racial subordination to economics. Rather, it must examine how people relate to the processes and struggles over the control of the means of production and reproduction. Such an inquiry reveals the exploitative character of the current social formation and the nature of individual and collective action developed around questions of individual and collective identity and social practice. No doubt, economic relations and imperatives influence the production of racial and gender ideologies, just as gender and racial structures can be understood only in the context of a historically constituted set of economic formations. Integrative anti-racism must speak to working-class concerns (e.g., equity, poverty, class bias in institutional structures and educational practices) in a way that recognizes the intersections of difference.

The examination of relations between different social groups is not synonymous with the political project of explicating the reasons why these groups exist in the first place (see McAll 1992). In all social formations, dominant groups exert their power through the systematic reproduction of the sources of their economic and political advantage. The linkage between cultural, social and economic power ensures a sustaining of the hegemonic relationship which allows for the appropriation of the wealth, knowledge and property of a weaker group. Racism, sexism and classism are ideological practices developed through a false sense of superiority of certain members of society. Using the power of "public opinion," popular culture and religious teachings on morality to create "false senses" is a strategy of domination.

Admittedly, the mode of reproduction of racism, sexism, homophobia and so forth cannot be explained with reference to capitalism alone. While all social formations have been good at maintaining subordinate and dominant relations, it appears, however, that post-industrial economies have systematically cultivated relations of domination between and among social groups to serve particular material and ideological interests. West (1987) has asked for an understanding of how racist beliefs form part of the common-sense knowledge of various social formations, how racist ideologies operate in everyday practices and constructions of identities, how state bureaucratic structures continually regulate the lives of racial minorities in particular, and how those minorities resist state repression, domination and class exploitation. To respond to these questions, we have to examine how racism, capitalist patriarchy and other forms of gender and sexual oppression work jointly in the lived experiences of people (see Stasiulis 1990). We must be able to articulate an alternative form of global education that connects issues of global economic oppression, capitalist patriarchy, human rights, environmental racism and international development, and respond to the urgent need to build coalitions across national borders to deal with global social injustice. Such global education will stress the mutual interdependence and interconnections among nations and peoples in a common struggle for change.

The question today is not whether capitalist social formations need racism and other oppressions to reproduce wealth and material advantage for their most privileged members. It is a question of *how* and *why*. Racism and patriarchy continue to be powerful ideologies and social practices that serve the interests of modern industrial capital (see Williams 1964). Racism, sexism and other forms of oppression, constituted along the lines of difference, function as effective social barriers. These practices help segment the labour force. As others have repeatedly argued, racism and sexism regulate the labour force not only by consigning people to particular roles and responsibilities in production relations, but also by the very practice of systemic exclusion from sharing in the material and social goods of society. But, above everything else, racism and other forms of oppression serve to maintain and reproduce the capitalist system.

Finally, the related *sixth* issue concerns how educators, students and community workers can engage in a progressive politics for *social transformation,* utilizing the integrative anti-racism approach. A more genuinely integrative anti-racism approach to social change requires focusing on the utilization of the relative power and privilege constituted around notions of race, class, gender and sexuality, and prioritizing *all* forms of oppression. Privilege and oppression, as Dahan (1992: 48) points out, co-exist in our individual and collective lives. By virtue of one's race, social class, gender and sexual orientation, it is easier or more difficult to access the dominant culture and the associated economic and political capital in Euro-Canadian/American contexts.

In the struggle for social transformation, public policy must not be confused with political action and, conversely, action should be seen as a precursor to effective change. For change to take place, integrative anti-racism discourse and practice must be grounded in people's actual material conditions. The political, communicative and educational practices of integrative anti-racism call for people to work together to develop a "community of differences"; that is, a community in which our differences help to strengthen us collectively to develop some degree of a shared commitment to justice and social transformation. Social transformation is possible when solidarity is understood to mean constructing coalitions among and between difference, and coalitions come to be openly defined in terms of relations of power (see Joyce 1995b). Without a doubt, struggles against race, class, gender and sexuality discrimination generate distinct versions of what justice should look like (see Troyna and Vincent 1995). But the goal of coalition building is to educate each other so that there is, or can be, a common view of justice. The struggle against injustice implies a struggle for justice. We cannot, as a society, choose to ignore injustice.

As we struggle for change through the politics of an integrative anti-racism approach, we must continually guard against what Mohanty has observed as the "erosion of the politics of collectivity through the reformulation of race and difference in individualistic terms" (1990: 204). This means that definitions of identity should extend beyond references to personal experience and make connections with the wider community. We cannot reject the politics of identity and difference. And, we cannot simply engage in what can be called "politics of the moment" or situational politics. Integrative anti-racism must ground the new politics of change in an understanding of the history of colonialism and re-colonization, as well as of how global capital (through processes of economic domination) continually produce definitions of "valid" knowledge about ourselves and society.

The politics of integrative anti-racism change can start in the classroom, in the home, in the workplace and in community actions and groups. There are some pedagogical and communicative challenges to the pursuit of an integrative anti-racist perspective. As already discussed, there is always the temptation to prioritize race and overlook the embedded inequalities which flow from class, ethnicity, culture, gender, sexuality and religious and language disparities, many of which are refracted through the official and hidden curriculum of the school and society. Since anti-racism education has to deal simultaneously with race, class, gender and sexual orientation, the anti-racist pedagogue, trainer and/or activist should necessarily be anti-classist, anti-sexist and anti-homophobic in her or his social practices. For anti-racism teachers, an awareness of the link between personal identity, experience and authority is crucial.

There must be congruence between the theory and practice engaged by anti-racism educators and practitioners. For example, the teacher's theoretical viewpoint of anti-racism education and the classroom atmosphere (e.g., that of an anti-authoritarian, democratic environment) that is nurtured should be closely aligned in order to make change happen. This is particularly true in the context of an anti-racist pedagogy that questions privilege, attempts to create a critical and powerful voice for students and develops their sense of critical judgement, while at the same time attempting to provide an openness to teaching that is non-universalizing.

Notes

1. See the film, "My Beautiful Launderette," for a representation of these complex relations.
2. As groups are formulated and reformulated within different relations and categories there is an inevitable homogenizing of groups of people. Larger groups of people are grouped under broad terms. "The Global Economy" is one such term. This epithet constructs us all as being involved in a seamless world economy; all sharing and producing the material goods of our collective labour. Cultural differentiation is a concomitant social process. While we may all be part of "the global economy," certain factions of our society get singled out for not contributing to this world of plenty. Racist, sexist and classist ideologies mobilize popular sentiment against these "troublemakers" and every other group scrambles for a moral high ground. This is the negative side of cultural differentiation. There are also processes of cultural differentiation that serve to empower marginalized groups as they claim space in the public consciousness.
3. By "cultural sexism" I am referring to patriarchal tendencies and practices embedded in upholding certain cultural traditions that are disempowering to women.

Chapter Five
The Challenges of Inclusive Schooling and Education: Multicentric Curriculum and Pedagogy

This chapter examines some of the challenges of developing an inclusive curriculum in Euro-Canadian/American contexts, highlighting the specific role of African-centred knowledge and the natural congruence or connections with anti-racism education. I have made a political choice to use an African-centred approach as one of many possible centres to illustrate multicentric education. My agenda is to put forward an educational philosophy and practice that connects issues of inclusive anti-racism education with Afrocentricity. Afrocentricity can offer some important lessons to education in Euro-Canadian/American contexts with the emphasis on the values of group unity, mutuality, collective responsibility, community and social bonding. These values can help move education away from an emphasis on individual competitiveness and a privileging of rights of individuals without any matching social responsibilities. The chapter is more than a philosophical treatise. I am interested in the development of an inclusive curriculum as a practical goal.

The discussion in this chapter is grounded in some specific personal experiences of the challenges and the constraints that the search for inclusivity poses to the status quo in Canadian schooling. I recall in my early days as a "foreign" graduate student in a Canadian post-secondary institution some of the subtle nuances and messages that made me at times feel "inadequate" and wanting to be "included." I vividly remember an advertisement on a notice board in the cafeteria which invited "international students" to enroll in English conversation classes, saying "guaranteed to lose your accents." For one thing, I did not have the money to enroll in these classes. But I also know the agonizing time I spent debating whether enrolling in the program would be beneficial for me in the long run if I were to "make it" in Canada. Interestingly, the fact that my accent could eventually end up being one of the things that readily identifies me as a Ghanaian-born and an African person did not cross my mind as something positive at the time.

Today, as I enjoy the privilege of teaching in one of Canada's foremost institutions of higher learning, I see the struggle for inclusivity being continually waged all around me. Increasingly, many of my graduate students, particularly minority students, are challenging educators to be more inclusive in their pedagogies and other educational practices. The message I keep hearing from the students is that something is not right with the academy, from its constructed hierarchies to the privileging of certain voices and the practices that lead to students' disengagement from school. The struggle and concern for inclusivity is being waged beyond the academy.[1]

More recently, I experienced another powerful educational moment. In the spring of 1992, I was organizing a panel session on "African Studies in Canada: Problems and Prospects in the Coming Decades" for the annual meeting of the Canadian Association of African Studies, to be held at the Université du Québec at Montréal. One of the most intelligent and articulate graduate students I have ever known, Handel Kashope Wright, who is of African descent, proposed a title for his paper presentation on the panel. It read: "We Would Rather be Reading Wole Soyinka." It was an indirect reference to an over-emphasis on the work of White, male, heterosexual literary scholars, and a yearning to be familiarized with non-European literary scholars. Recently, Handel Wright, during one of our academic engagements, reminded me that most Canadian educational institutions of higher learning do not need a sign in front of their buildings to indicate that they are Eurocentric, patriarchal and, thus, systematically oppressive institutions. The environment, culture and organizational life in many western institutions provide enough experiences to allow non-Western individuals to reach such conclusions (see Chilungu and N'iang 1989).

I remember attending a monthly meeting of the Organization of Parents of Black Children (OPBC) in Toronto in the summer of 1992. A discussion about empowering Black/African-Canadian youth to do well in school touched on the importance of teaching Black/African history to students. I remember vividly one parent posing a question to the effect that, while he understood the importance of teaching about Black/African history, he was unsure what Black/African history could do for those youths who are failing mathematics and science subjects in school. Another parent replied that she was unsure, herself, about the right answer to this question. However, she felt certain about one thing: if children can relate to what they are learning, they learn better. She added further, "I know this from my own experience." At the end of the meeting, parents agreed that, at the very least, educators should focus their students on mathematics and science classes and problem-solving. They should discuss the contributions of Black scientists to the development of these fields in order to assure their students that they are equally capable of making similar contributions. Such an education strategy points to the need to change the content of mathematics and science courses.

A final relevant experience occurred in the winter of 1994 when a Toronto newspaper carried a front-page caption that read, "Home in Cuffs." There was a photograph of a Black male who was returned to Canada to face murder charges after escaping to the United States. He had allegedly killed his White Canadian girlfriend at a university campus. The caption "Home in Cuffs" struck me in many ways. I wondered whether all Canadians saw Canada as "home" for this Black male. There are many Whites who often insinuate that all non-Whites are "immigrants" from "elsewhere"; to call this "home" for the Black male was interesting. Razack has pointed out that the category of "immigrant" "easily slides into the more racialized construct of foreigner" (1995a: 68) and is usually invoked to serve powerful interests in society. African-Canadian writer, Marlene Nourbese Philip, in a piece in *The Toronto Star* also observed that for many of those so labelled the term "immigrant" has become a perpetual definition.[2] Reflecting on the headline in the newspaper, I said to myself, of course there is a larger project going on here. The image fits well into the conventional media's disturbing portrayals of Black youth as "violent," "trouble-makers" and as "criminals." Equally important for Black youth, the word "home" is used to instill fear as it subtextually alludes to "deportation" and going "home to face the music."

These experiences are significant educational moments. In particular, they speak in diverse ways to how the issues of race identity and representation are important in both public discourses and political debates. A knowledge of the disaffection of some students with the Euro-Canadian/American school system is crucial to politically contextualize academic debates about inclusive schooling. In fact, within the Canadian context, an extensive amount of research data exist on the "problems" and issues of minority education in general. However, as Daenzer and Dei (1994) point out, research by race is still an unsettling issue for many Canadians. Disaggregating research into issues affecting specifically African-Canadian youth is relatively new to Canada. This is notwithstanding the common-sense knowledge of the connections between race identity, representation and education.

Fortunately, in the broader Euro-American contexts, there is a wide body of research that shows significant differences in the schooling experiences of minority youth, particularly Black youth and those of Asian background (see Carby 1982b; Oliver 1986; Amos and Parmar 1987; Comer 1988; Fine 1991; Garibaldi 1992; Jacob and Jordan 1993; Ernst and Statzner 1994; Ernst, Statzner and Trueba 1994; Alladin 1995). To varying degrees, this growing body of data shows that the structural processes of schooling and education provide unequal opportunities and create differential outcomes for students according to race, ethnicity, gender and class. Many of these works speak to the racial, cultural and gender "othering" of students. For example, in the schools, the social construction of "deviance" is derived from patriarchal relations of schooling. What has so far been constructed as the norm is the androcentric worldview, and schools are accordingly structured around male organizational modes. Arguably, dominant discourses around some youth in the wider society define the meanings and stereotypes that many educators apply to those youths in their schools. Disaffected students complain about the school and off-school environment and what they perceive as a lack of opportunities to realize their dreams and ambitions. For minority students in particular, the nuances of their shifting identities and intersecting marginalities are exacerbated by the failure of the education system to recognize that all students enter classrooms with a reservoir of cultural and political capital. When minority students, for example, utilize such capital to resist hegemonic norms and values and patriarchal structures that they perceive as subordinating them even further, students are labelled "deviant," "problem children" and "at-risk youth."

It is not refreshing to note that many educators are still grappling with a comprehensive understanding of how race and the relational aspects of difference (ethnicity, class, gender, sexuality) affect the schooling and educational outcomes of youth. This situation of educators is a concern at the heart of the struggle for inclusive schooling. The struggle demands that an educator is willing to be a "voice of difference." By that I mean willing to challenge the status quo by rupturing the racialized, hetero-patriarchal nature of educational settings and the prevailing culture of dominance. To succeed in the task, educators will have to generate alternative approaches in the classroom (and sometimes oppositional initiatives) to achieve inclusive schooling and education.

Inclusive Schooling

Inclusive schooling refers to educational practices that make for genuine inclusion of *all* students by addressing equity issues and promoting successful learning outcomes, particularly for students of racial and ethnic minority backgrounds (Dei and Razack 1995). Inclusive schooling is making "excellence" accessible to all students. Of equal significance, the idea of inclusive schooling seeks to develop schools into "working communities" and to bring the notions of "community" and "social responsibility" into the centre of public schooling in Euro-Canadian/American contexts.

Dealing with our social, economic, cultural, sexuality and class (for example) differences is the key to inclusive schooling and education. To many anti-racist educators the notion of "inclusivity" in the school system means:

1. Dealing foremost with *equity*; that is, dealing with the qualitative value of justice.
2. Addressing the question of *representation*; that is, having a multiplicity of perspectives entrenched as part of the academic discourse, knowledge and texts.
3. Making school instructional practices respond to the challenges of *diversity*: that is, responding to the social construction and structuralization of difference

(e.g., issues of race, class, gender, sexual orientation, age and ability) within the school system and in the wider society.

In effect, inclusive schooling means opening spaces for alternative and, sometimes, oppositional paradigms to flourish in the schools. It means ensuring representation of diverse populations in the schools. It means developing a broad-based curriculum and diverse teaching strategies, and having support systems in the schools that enhance the conditions for success for all students. I agree with Peter McLaren when he says, "diversity must be affirmed within a politics of cultural criticism and a commitment to social justice," and also, that difference must be validated as "a product of history, culture, power and ideology" (Estrada and McLaren 1993: 31).

The Deep Curriculum

The starting point for developing an inclusive curriculum is for educators to acknowledge that racism, sexism, homophobia, classism and ableism are integral parts of Canadian society. We must privilege and not devalue diversity and difference in conceptualizing what may be characterized as the "deep curriculum" (Holmes and Mazzuca 1995). The term "deep curriculum" is used here to refer to both the official and hidden aspects of the school curricula (for the Canadian school context see Mukherjee and Thomas n.d.: 7), as well as the intersections of the school culture, environment and relations of power among educators, students and parents. Curriculum, in this context, includes the experiences that students bring to school (Kugler 1995a). It is important to note that such a broad definition of the curriculum would also include both stipulated and unspoken school rules and regulations that influence student and staff activities, behaviours, attitudes, perceptions, expectations and outcomes (e.g., school calendars, celebrations, food services, assemblies, concerts, athletics, bulletins, hallway displays). These elements constitute the school's personality or character and present students with the "acceptable" values and standards of the school (see Bhyat 1993: 12; Mukherjee and Thomas n.d.: 7).

Inclusive schooling means first and foremost the adoption of "deep curriculum." A discussion of the "deep curriculum" is a discourse about the structures and/or environments within which the learning, teaching and administration of education take place within the schools. Theoretically, this would be an interrogation of existing power relations within schools which serve to entrench hegemonic ideas and interests of dominant groups. Philosophically, it is also a critique that links concerns for an inclusive schooling with calls for anti-racism education. Like anti-racism education, inclusive schooling should be seen as, or within, the context of an educational agenda to reform every aspect of the school system so as to reflect the diverse concerns, interests and aspirations which make up our society.

While issues of inclusiveness address inequalities within the school, equally important is the impact of the system reforms upon the wider society. We must be deeply concerned about the society/communal implications (see Radwanski 1987). While these issues are beyond the scope of this chapter, we must not lose sight of the fact that we are concerned here with the potential for social transformation. Implicit within our discussion is the recognition that deep curriculum changes foster greater student participation and lead to greater societal involvement in practices and experiences which allow positive schooling experiences to be transferred into positive adult participation.

Existing critical studies on the education of Canadian minority youth problematize the absence of an inclusive school environment (see Board of Education 1988; Braithwaite 1989; James 1990; CABE 1992; Solomon 1992; Daenzer and Dei 1994; Dei, Holmes, Mazzuca, McIsaac and Campbell 1995; Dei and Razack 1995). This critique is not new. Many so-called immigrant parents have complained over the years that Canadian schools have not provided a complete understanding of what it means to live in a pluralistic society (see Lewis 1992). For example, in the province of Ontario, one can point to a long history of community and parental involvement in encouraging the public school system to address concerns about diversity and inclusivity. Historically, so-called immigrant parents and community workers have organized and demanded structural changes to address concerns about discrimination and prejudice in the schools, and worked for policy and curriculum changes at the school board level (see Brand and Bhaggiyadatta 1986; Dehli, Restakis and Sharpe 1988). Such local community efforts were instrumental in the establishment of race-relations policies and heritage-language programs during the regular school day in many school boards (e.g., in Ontario, Nova Scotia, New Brunswick) in the early 1980s. A few school boards in Ontario have since instituted committees to examine school curriculum for any bias. These have been important victories but they can also be co-opted by the school board machinery to prevent them from destabilizing the educational system.

The present struggle for inclusive Canadian schools has a proud history. In Canada, the historic struggles of local community groups, parents and students for inclusive curriculum and educational equity are not limited to Ontario (see D'Oyley 1994). There are the well-documented historic struggles in Nova Scotia, New Brunswick and Vancouver. In Nova Scotia the struggles of local groups for school inclusivity provided inspiration for the Parent-Student Association at Preston after the Cole Harbour conflict in the 1980s (Calliste 1994b).[3] The Association also initiated the African-Canadian Educational Project which developed Afrocentric curriculum for its Saturday school. This initiative has been piloted in other areas. There are also the initiatives of the Halifax-based Black Learners' Advisory Committee for multicultural and anti-racism education in schools, colleges and universities to promote Black learning (see Calliste 1994c).

It is generally argued that the lack of an inclusive school environment makes it difficult for marginalized minority youth to develop a sense of identification with, and connectedness to, their schools. There has been some recognition of this fact at the provincial governmental level. In 1995 the Nova Scotia government announced funding for the development of a new curriculum in Halifax schools that will include courses on Black history, culture and traditions. In the fall of 1995 the Ministry of Education in New Brunswick announced the development of a new policy on race relations to cover changes in curriculum and teacher-training (see Lewington 1995). In Ontario, a number of policy initiatives have been taken, particularly in the 1990s, ostensibly to respond to minority education issues (see Wright and Allingham 1994). Four most notable policy documents, *The Common Curriculum* (Ministry of Education and Training [MET] 1993a), *Anti-Racism and Ethnocultural Equity in School Boards. Guidelines for Policy Development and Implementation* (MET 1993b), *Changing Perspectives: A Resource Guide for Race and Ethnocultural Equity Education—All Divisions and OACS* (Ontario Ministry of Education OME 1992) and *Violence-Free Schools* (MET 1993c) are aimed directly and indirectly at meeting the challenge for inclusivity. While these policies have been devised with the best of intentions, there is still the difficulty of translating well-meaning policy documents into concrete plans of action. Due to the absence of appropriate guidelines, accountability for these issues has often been left to the discretion of individual school boards or school principals. Often, school boards and educators have also complained about the lack of resources to implement many of these government policies. What this means to the student is that strategies for increased staff representation and curriculum diversity have still not been implemented to affect educational outcomes. At the present time, no one knows what will happen to these policies given the election of a right wing Conservative government in Ontario in the summer of 1995.

The Notion of "Multi-Centric Education"

Enhancing the curriculum and making it inclusive for all students is a noble objective. But there comes a point when "enhancement" and mere "inclusion" may not be enough. We should begin to ask, what is in this educational initiative/approach for specific groups who continue to exist on the margins of the school system despite the good intentions of inclusivity? How do we respond to the crisis of education, "dropping out" and "underachievement" for certain identifiable groups in the school system? These questions recognize the unevenness of the playing field and the fact that we cannot engage in conversations about "inclusiveness" as if all students come to school on an equal footing.

For example, in North America, it is generally conceded that the "dropout" problem is acute among certain social groups (e.g., Blacks and First Nations). In a 1991 high school survey by one board of education in Ontario, it was revealed that African-Canadian youth were not doing as well as other students in terms of credit accumulation. It was shown that 36 percent of Black students were "at risk" of dropping out because of failure to accumulate sufficient credits to graduate within six years. This compared with 26 percent for Whites and 18 percent for Asians (see Yau, Cheng and Ziegler 1993; Cheng 1995). This survey also confirmed "that 45% of Black high-school students were enrolled in the Basic and General levels, compared to 28% of the entire student body placed in those two lower streams" (Cheng 1995: 2; see also Cheng, Tsuji, Yau and Ziegler 1993: 15; Brown, Cheng, Yau and Ziegler 1992: 13).[4] In the most revealing statistics, the board's study of high school students who enrolled in 1987 showed that by 1991, 42 percent of Black students (compared to the overall student population, across all groups of 33 percent) dropped out of school (see Brown 1993: 5). A similar disturbing picture was noted for Portuguese students (41 percent). These figures can be compared to the low dropout rate of Asian students (18 percent), and the 31 percent rate for White students.

In light of such unflattering statistics, I do not see any pedagogic or communicative error in espousing the notion of a "multi-centric education" if that means targeting groups for attention and centring the lived experiences of a diverse student body as a starting point for education. Many racial minority youth have to contend with a dominance of "Whiteness" in the schools that, historically, has left no room for alternative ideas to flourish. The danger of Eurocentricity is that it is the only centre; it is presented as the only valid knowledge form through the constant devaluation and delegitimation of other forms of ideas. It is this process which is systemic in formal education. It is a structural process whereby minority youths' language and culture are devalued. In fact, one of the original purposes of public education was to assimilate new Canadians through educational transformation. It was believed that the maintenance of a minority language and culture was a hindrance to assimilation and therefore should be mitigated (Rahim 1990). An extreme example of this can be found in the Aboriginal residential schools. Yet the Eurocentric approach has only fostered greater student marginalization and leads ultimately to fading out.[5] This has given rise to the necessity of centring students within the curriculum.

Thus, while in principle I subscribe to a theory of an inclusive curriculum, like hooks (1984, 1990) I am talking about the marginalized moving from the margins to the centre, and not simply being grafted into the existing order. This is important because current definitions and practices of "inclusion" do not go far enough; they still leave people on the margins even when all are supposedly included. There is also what appears to be a shift away from blatant exclusion to selective inclusion (see Behdad 1993). An example is the tendency to offer a few courses dealing with minority themes in the course syllabus and to interpret and understand such initiatives as creating genuinely inclusive schooling (see Swartz 1992; King 1992). Furthermore, as already argued, anti-racism is about a redefinition of power structures and the rupturing of asymmetric relations of domination and power in society, rather than an insertion into existing patriarchal structures. In this context, to paraphrase Daigre (1994), the goal of inclusive education is to bring all minority students onto the stage of the school drama as major actors, not merely as players supporting an all-White European cast.

In this political context, it is perhaps more appropriate to talk about a search for a *balanced curriculum*, rather than simply an inclusive curriculum. The idea of a "balance" is predicated on arriving at some "centrality" in terms of how students situate themselves and their cultures, histories and experiences in the learning process. In other words, centrality is a matter of locating students within the context of their own cultural frame of reference so that they can relate socially, politically, ideologically, spiritually and emotionally to the learning process (see Asante 1991: 171).

The struggle against hegemonic knowledge is not simply an attempt to do away with centric forms of knowledge. The idea of centric education should not be confused with hegemonic education. There is no natural connection between the two practices; thus, any connection should be challenged and resisted. Given the historical dominance of Eurocentric knowledge, what is required are additional forms of centric knowledge that empower minority youth in particular to counter their history of being treated as inferior in Euro-Canadian/American school systems. Having a multicentric education could have the effect of actually decentring spaces in the classroom for all participants such that there are many centres. The idea of a "centre" loses its powerful meaning of exclusion when it is only one of several centres. The unfortunate contemporary reality is that, to be able to challenge effectively the dominance of Eurocentric education, there must be room in our schools for alternative and oppositional knowledge systems to flourish.

Developing an Inclusive Multi-Centric Curriculum: Asking the Right Questions

The task of developing an inclusive curriculum begins with educators asking critical questions about themselves, the schools and society in general. There are questions around the broad themes of race, class, sexual and gender equity, as well as pedagogical and educational practices of teachers and schools. For example, educators and those who subscribe to their ideas of transformative learning need to ask:

1. Do all students have equal access to available resources and materials in the school setting?
2. What is taught in the schools?
3. What is not taught? What are the omissions, negations and misrepresentations in the existing texts?
4. What should be taught, by whom and how?
5. Who wields the ultimate power to make the above (question 4) and other school decisions?
6. What is the political project behind introducing an equity curriculum and for

engaging in an "equity pedagogy" (Hilliard 1992)?

7. How do educators create a genuinely democratic learning environment for all students?
8. Do the teaching styles used engage and equip students with the critical thinking skills needed to question all aspects of the "deep curriculum?"
9. How are minorities, women and the poor portrayed?
10. What is being exoticized, totalized or essentialized, and by whom and how?
11. How are questions of power, privilege, oppression and inequality acknowledged and dealt with?
12. What voices, opinions and experiences are being heard? Who is being silenced and how?
13. What responsibilities are being denied?
14. Do the teaching strategies used help students to critically review classroom discourses for their implications for race, ethnicity, class, age, physical ability, gender and sexual orientation?
15. How do educators prepare students to deal with the contradiction between the school's promise of equality and the realities of racism, sexism and other forms of oppression and inequality in society?
16. How do educators affirm differences in their schools?
17. Do educators see the cultures that students bring to school as a source of "cultural enrichment" or as "cultural baggage?"
18. How do educators assist students to create their own visibility in the schools?
19. Do educators relate to each student as an individual or as a member of a group?
20. How do educators, students and staff occupy and share non-hegemonic spaces?

These questions are by no means exhaustive. I also do not profess to have answers for all of them. But, it is important to note that critical teaching moves beyond a mere recognition of difference to involve responding meaningfully and concretely to differences (see Greene 1994; Valli 1994; King 1994). In fact, classroom teachings need to recognize the power of lived experience, experiences of difference, and the relevance of what is taught and learned to the material conditions of everyday existence in society (Greene 1994). Teachers can engage in issues-oriented teaching to help students recognize social oppression and institutionalized inequality and determine how to act conscientiously to address and remove social injustice.

The issue of inclusive, anti-racist schooling transcends the calls for curriculum and pedagogic reforms. It calls for engaging in the task of structurally transforming schools to ensure that the faces of school decision-makers reflect the diversity of our larger population. Fundamentally, it calls for a transformation of power relations in the schools. It calls for creating spaces for alternative and oppositional knowledge to flourish and not be marginalized. It calls for new ways of thinking about schooling and education. It calls for challenging status quoism in the schools and society, starting from the individual and collective strength of those pushing for change. These are the concerns that guide teacher preparation for inclusive schooling.

Teacher Preparation and Inclusive Schooling

Key to building a truly inclusive school is a transformation of the conventional curriculum. One cannot talk about inclusive schooling or even a balanced curriculum without reforming existing teaching, pedagogic and communicative practices. We need new and alternative teaching and learning practices that initially help students in diverse school settings to critically re-read and re-think how Eurocentric knowledge is reproduced through negation, omission, denigration and misrepresentation of alternative ways of knowing. A problem is that educational critics may be asking some teachers to teach in ways and/or to perform in settings for which they have not been duly trained. Not every teacher in the current school system has the skills and knowledge to interrogate the status quo and question why things are the way they are. In fact, not surprisingly, some teachers justify "inequality and exploitation by accepting the existing order of things as given" (King 1991: 135). Thus it is important for all teachers to develop an understanding of the basic principles of anti-racism education. Anti-racism teacher-training could ensure that the questions listed above are appreciated and acted upon in non-threatening ways.

There are additional understandings which are key for teachers engaging in anti-racism education. The first is an understanding of the multiple roles that individuals occupy in the school system and society, and how knowledge, social power and economic privilege work in mutually reinforcing ways to structure people's daily lives. Contemporary educators should be able to critically examine the nature of patriarchal relations and male organizational modes of schooling and to call into question how schools function to establish hierarchies (see Kugler 1995a: 13). In dealing with the male-centric power structures of schools, teachers should be able to work with their students to develop alternative structures and strategies for curriculum transformation and for students and local community involvement in the running of schools.

A related concern is that all educators and students have some understanding of how schools reproduce inequality. This would make it possible to effectively challenge all forms of social oppression. If anti-racism education is to succeed in transforming schools, an appropriate model for an inclusive curriculum would be the pedagogic approach which best enables educators and schools to teach students about the structural inequities in the schools and society (see Sleeter and Grant 1987: 434–6). Schools can begin by examining how administrative practices marginalize, exclude and alienate some groups and place others at a social disadvantage (practices such as streaming, testing procedures and the absence of minority teachers within the system). These practices can then be challenged.

A second concern is that collaboration be pursued diligently as a major goal in contemporary education. Teachers should be able to uphold and promote strategies for co-operative learning which also emphasize collaboration and bonding among students, administrators, teachers and parents. Teacher preparation could be geared towards helping schools cultivate effective social relations between and within them in a mutually supporting environment. Such an environment would allow for meaningful dialogue and collaborative work between and among teachers, administrators, students, parents and community workers. It would be possible for teachers, administrators and students to network to develop a community of learners and educators. Classroom teaching, for example, would stress the development of social networks and global interdependence and show how economic, social and political issues are connected across local, regional, national and international boundaries. Classroom teaching could also cover the implications of education for peace, environmental safety and the protection of human rights and freedoms (also International Institute for Global Education [IIGE] 1995) .

To address the critical question of what should be taught in the schools and how, educators should be able to devise and implement alternative instructional strategies that provide students with group and collaborative learning skills, and the ability to identify and solve basic human problems. The curriculum and classroom instructional practice could allow students to set their own priorities for their learning. Curriculum and pedagogy could be adaptable to the local environment and the interests and activities of students and broader community goals. Teaching an inclusive curriculum as praxis could allow students to examine their own educational histories and their experiences of living in communities and relating to one another. It could also allow students to question authority and the discretionary use of power.

A third key concern is that anti-racism teacher education cannot be effective if teachers and schools do not value the congruence between anti-racism principles and practices (see IIGE 1995). As a form of political education, an inclusive pedagogy means teaching students to follow through on what is learned. Educators lead by setting appropriate examples. Students should not feel any dissonance in terms of what their teachers speak about theoretically in the classroom, and what they actually do outside the school walls. Progressive educators practise what they preach (e.g., matching their theoretical exhortations against oppression, their intellectual criticism of social injustice and their political affirmation of social difference with community political action). As Kugler also points out, appreciating the correlation between principles and practices ensures "honesty and makes everything else have real meaning" (1995a: 28)

Fourth, teachers can lead the way to resurrect the "subjugated knowledges" (Foucault 1980: 81) of their students. Classroom instruction could encourage students to find their own voices. Progressive educators would join with students to challenge the peripheralizing of alternative and oppositional viewpoints, perspectives and discourses within school knowledge. Such pedagogues could ensure that minority students' voices and experiences are brought from the fringes into mainstream academic discourses and school experiences. Educators should engage students to speak from their various social locations to articulate alternative views to form counter-definitions to those portrayed in the curriculum (see Estrada and McLaren 1993). The critical pedagogue always assists students to explore alternative and oppositional forms of knowledge informed by their own histories and experiences. As Peter McLaren argues, an affirmation of the voices (and legitimation of the experiences) of students and the oppressed in the classroom discourse allows students to undertake a critical reading of school texts and to create their own alternative and oppositional forms of knowledge (Estrada and McLaren 1993: 32; see also Banks 1994a: 6; Byrne 1994: 10).

The fifth consideration is that teaching should assist students in learning about the achievements of all groups in a way that addresses questions of inclusivity and the validation of alternative knowledges. Students should know about the achievements and contributions of the diverse social groups that make up Euro-Canadian/American society. Such education would not be conducted in a piecemeal fashion or discussed largely from the oppressor's stance. A holistic approach to such education highlights the moments and sites of political resistance to enslavement, domination and subjugation. Rather than adopting a celebratory approach to different ethnic histories, students and teachers would make connections to how the historic achievements and contributions of different ethnic groups are in fact central to Canadian/American history as a whole. Students should also be encouraged to critically examine these histories and contributions and learn from any past mistakes.

The sixth concern is that teachers know what to do with available resource materials. This issue goes beyond legitimate questions of relevancy to availability and knowing how to access and use resource materials. There are questions, such as what is the educator's response and approach to racist, sexist, classist, homophobic, and so forth, materials/texts, and what are the appropriate models and/or approaches for developing an inclusive curriculum? While arguments have been made for using texts that are biased against minority groups to teach critically, educators should balance this approach with some concern for the pain and the hurt feelings of students.

A seventh component of anti-racism education is that teachers should be able to recognize students, parents, community workers and care-givers as genuine partners in the production and dissemination of school and social knowledge. Local community knowledge is an important pedagogical tool and source of cultural information which educators can tap for the benefit of their students and the school. Educators must find ways to involve community workers, parents, guardians and care-givers in their teaching practices. For example, schools would create space for members of the local community to walk in, share ideas and teach students.[6]

The final concern is that educational strategies to address problems of exclusion in the school system target *all* students, teachers and staff. Curriculum design, reform and management should have input from all stakeholders in the educational system. An inclusive anti-racism approach to education seeks to rupture the school "deep curriculum" and transform it (not as an additive solution). A primary objective of the structural change of the current school system should be to allow students to develop some sense of responsibility to a larger global citizenry. But this can only be possible if all students are allowed to see themselves throughout the "deep curriculum." This is precisely what African-centred education aims for, with its starting/entry point to, and target audience of, students of Black/African ancestry. African-centred education provides an example of an effective approach that seeks to ensure that students of African descent, in particular (but not exclusively), connect issues of culture, identity, politics and history in schooling and education.

Towards One Model of Inclusive Anti-Racism Education: African-Centred Knowledge and Inclusive Schooling

Let me state at the outset that my use of the term "Black/African" in this context is not in refeence exclusively to skin colour, but refers generally to the political sense of peoples who have collectively been disadvantaged by systems of colonialism and imperialism. This interpretation does not preclude the usage of the term that targets peoples who claim descent from Africa nor who identify with the political history of the continent. The anti-racism educational project focuses on the emotional and intellectual development of Black peoples that were destroyed by the processes of colonization and its aftermath. I am also discussing African-centred education and its connections with anti-racism *not* from a disinterested perspective. Furthermore, the focus is not intended to prioritize African-centred knowledge over other ways of knowing. As pointed out, it is important that the discussion be seen in the context of the political and academic need to create spaces for a plurality of perspectives and sometimes oppositional knowledge to flourish. African-centred knowledge is one window through which to view the philosophy and practice of multicentric curriculum and pedagogy. It is important to reiterate my philosophical position that curriculum in schools must be diversified so that programing is culture-specific without marginalizing minority cultures. It is also important that transformative educational strategies and curricular practices strive to reflect the indigenousness of those involved, particularly the ideas they propose (see Swartz 1992: 342).

Questions relating to African-centred education may also be asked about the pursuit of First Nations-centred, Asian-centred and other forms of anti-racism education in Euro-Canadian/American contexts. Let me use questions about First Nations education to illustrate this point because it is an important centre in North American schooling and education. In fact, speaking from the Euro-

Canadian/American stage, Aboriginal education is the initial centre. In discussions on inclusive schooling, it is legitimate to ask what do Euro-Canadian/American schools offer the youth by way of indigenous education and knowledge (see Zarate 1994)? Is there room for First Nations/Aboriginal knowledge in the current processes of schooling and education in Euro-Canadian/American contexts? Is it possible for First Nations peoples to communicate and relate spiritually with other peoples with different worldviews in the current school system of North America? The formal education system based on the colonial model has not responded to the concerns, needs and aspirations of First Nations peoples in North America (see Battiste and Barman 1995; Perrott-Lightning 1995). This fact is attested to, for example, by the alarming school dropout rates for First Nations students (see Mackay and Myles 1989, 1995). The grave underrepresentation of First Nations scholars in Canadian colleges and universities is also common knowledge (see Grant 1995).

Without a doubt there is a place for the indigenous knowledges of Aboriginal peoples to be taught in the schools. Unfortunately, traditional knowledge of the indigenous peoples of North America have not been fully analyzed for their contributions to education in North America. Schools have failed to promote indigenous education and knowledge as legitimate and alternative ways of knowing. The situation is complicated by what Yarmol-Franko (1992: 4) has identified as the chasm existing between Aboriginal and Western thought, and the fact that certain ideas of Aboriginal peoples cannot be appropriately transmitted within the frames of Western knowledge systems.

It is a question of creating a space for a synthesis of different knowledges to take place to serve the needs of education in Euro-Canadian/American contexts. First Nations peoples can and do generate knowledge about their own societies that any initiative for inclusive schooling could do well to tap. There has to be a space for such discussion to take place in the schools in conjunction with other non-Western systems of thought or forms of education. We cannot dismiss the fact that Asiacentric, Eurocentric and Afrocentric worldviews, among others, each contain educationally relevant values and ideas that can be tapped to provide some solutions to global problems (see Keto 1990). At this political juncture, in light of the crisis for African youth with respect to education, I have chosen to dwell on African-centred knowledge, cognizant of the need for a synthesis of different worldviews as they relate to the delivery of education and knowledge in North America.

I contend that designing one model of anti-racism education for all peoples will ultimately fail, for it would mean disallowing the particular histories and experiences of various groups of people. Simply put, an anti-racism education for Whites must indeed be different from that of Blacks because both groups have historically been placed in vastly different positions in the mechanics of social oppression. But, if anti-racism entails the exposure and learning of new knowledge for all, then we need to consider seriously the implications of African-centred knowledge and other forms of alternative pedagogy for a broad strategy of anti-racism education.

Wright (1994) correctly points to the possible marginalization of African-centred knowledge in the academy if the Afrocentric discourse is strictly self-referential. Thus, African-centred education must seek to construct an alliance with other critical theories and to articulate an emancipatory pedagogy that has resonance for all students. This entails placing African-centred knowledge within the anti-racism approach to educational change in the schools. This means highlighting both the intersections and the congruence between the two frames of reference, and the possibilities for political education to effect meaningful change that will disrupt current power relations.

My academic and political project is to resolve how a non-hegemonic African-centred knowledge can be incorporated in school teachings for the benefit of all students. My argument is that Euro-Canadian/American schools need a new form of education that will particularly assist Black youth to reinvent their Africanness within a Diasporic context, and create a way of being and thinking that is congruent with positive African traditions and values. The rationale, as Lee-Ferdinand argues, is that "Eurocentrism has been insidious in its universality, creating a common alienation among all African peoples" (1994: 12).

Hunter (1983) cautioned that to argue that one's social reality is the only reality is the most dangerous of all delusions. Discussion of African-centred education raises concern around the issue of linking identity to schooling and around the importance of culture in schooling and education for the youth. As already argued, the notion of identity requires that educators draw on the cultures and ancestry of their students. This does not mean that educators construct monolithic identities. Social identities are transient, invoking the powerful notion of "hybridity" (Bhabha 1991, 1994). To a large measure, social criticisms of identity-based knowledge have focused on the fact that such knowledge does not speak to the experiences of every member in the socially constructed group. Those who identify in particular ways with specific cultural or geographical borders should be able to articulate social identities that speak directly to their experiential realities, without necessarily having to defend the universality of such experiences. Those who do not identify with such defined spaces should be able to articulate a historical narrative that speaks to the continuum of human experiences, allows for fluid definitions of positionality and makes powerful sense of the notions of hybridity in post-modern contexts. I am also reminded by a subheading in a recent piece on "The Choices of Identity" by Denis-Constant Martin that "we are all cultural hybrids" (1995: 16).

Cultural identity, like racial identity, is a powerful aspect of social life. Individuals should be able to articulate their affiliations with social groups of their choice at the same time as society continually defines and classifies people. The increasing cultural heterogeneity, reconfigurations of cultural borders and geographical spaces, and the "redefinitions of local and global relations, and the constitution of subjects" have resulted in a contestation of identities in diverse social environments (Goldberg and Zegeye 1995: 1). The ability to define self and group identities provides an important political and cultural knowledge base from which to fight social racism and other forms of collective injustices.

The discussion of African-centred knowledge is not intended to essentialize the identities of the Black population in the school system. The Black student population is not a homogenous group. Students may not share the same need for African-centred education just because they are Black. Educational research has shown that there are certain issues around which concerns of Continental African students, Caribbean-born students and Canadian-born students of African descent converge and diverge. Even these groupings are heterogeneous populations. In my own study of Black youths' experiences in Ontario, it was found that students' concerns vary to some extent (Dei, Holmes, Mazzuca, McIsaac and Campbell 1995). For example, Continental African students have concerns about the broad issues of language, religion and culture. Students who have been schooled in the Caribbean complain about the "social labelling" of Black students as "trouble-makers." Black people from other regions share this concern. There are also complaints about the attempts by schools to place students from the Caribbean in English skills development (ESD) classes. Pointed questions of identity are raised by students born here in Canada and, particularly, to mixed parents. These students often wonder why a part of their identity is denied when they are expected to self-identify as Black. Furthermore, these students, even though they were born in Canada, still have to respond to questions about "where are you from?" just because for the most part they are socially constructed as Black (see Dei, Holmes, Mazzuca, McIsaac and Campbell 1995). However, it is noted that the differential treatment, the lack of representation of Black/African perspectives, histories and experiences, the absence of Black teachers, and a prevailing culture of White, Eurocentric dominance in the mainstream school system are concerns shared by all Black youth. These concerns serve to ensure that diverse students of African heritage can relate to basic tenets of African-centred education.

Some have questioned whether Canadian- or Caribbean-born students of African descent identify with Africa at all. If, in fact, these students do not identify with Africa, it is important to attribute the cause to the intense dose of negativity about the continent that mainstream school and popular media discourses present to unsuspecting youth and the wider Canadian audience. For how can one talk of the Caribbean and not contextualize debates in the history of Africa and African peoples? The Caribbean cannot be fully understood and appreciated outside the context of a critical review of the history of Africa and African peoples and political economic developments of the Americas. Likewise, to understand the history of Africans in the Diaspora we have to recognize the links with Africa and the Caribbean. The significant historical events of slavery and colonialism continue to affect current developments on the African continent.

Making linkages between African peoples' histories, cultures and contemporary political developments in North America and Africa is important. To do so is not to deny Caribbean and African-Canadian histories and cultures in their own right. On the contrary, recognizing historical context enriches our understanding of African peoples as survivors, resistors and change agents.

The Afrocentric discourse is about a paradigm shift; it means teaching about an alternative way of knowing, informed by the histories and cultural experiences of all peoples of African descent. As a pedagogic and communicative tool, African-centred education calls on educators within Euro-Canadian/American school systems to centre their analysis and investigations of African and Black issues in a perspective grounded in African ways of knowing. The challenge, as Asante (1991) puts it, is to "move" or "bring" all peoples of African descent from the margins to the centre of post-modern history. For the educator, the challenge is to allow the African child to see and interpret the world with his or her own eyes, rather than with those of the "other."

African-centred education also calls for an awareness, on the part of the educator, of the social and political contexts of public schooling. This means that schooling is adapted to fit the differences which, for example, youth of African descent and other minorities bring to the school environment. More importantly, the anti-racism African-centred paradigm critiques a "liberal" ideology that fails to speak about and effect social change that disrupts the current power relations in the school setting. An African-centred pedagogy seeks to empower students and educators to question the dominant status quoism of an Eurocentric paradigm.

Many minority students in Euro-Canadian/American schools are faced with the enormous challenge of searching for their identities while struggling to identify with their school. These students are trying to escape social labels and to relate to a school system that has historically failed to teach youth about their cultural histories and heritage, and the contributions of their forebears to society. Minority students continue to occupy school environments where issues about the deep curriculum (e.g., climate, culture, instructional materials, pedagogical practices, texts) fail to centre their individual personhood, lived experiences and sense of membership in society. The failure to provide students with a sense of belonging to a cultural heritage explains the ambivalence some African-Canadian students may feel about identifying with their African roots.

The history of Africa clearly reveals that social resistance struggles have formed a greater part of the material conditions of human existence than the current images of misery, disease, hunger and poverty that are constantly fed to the Euro-Canadian/American public. The Afrocentric project views the Euro-Canadian/American school system as both part of the problem and the solution. Schools have an important role to play in helping the public unlearn many of the stereotypes about Africa and peoples of African descent. A key question is, how do educators, administrators and parents respond to the challenges of schooling and education in racially diverse, multi-ethnic communities? No doubt it requires multiple, overlapping and non-exclusive educational strategies. Hilliard has called for the "meaningful rendition of the whole human experience" (1992: 13) in the processes of schooling and education of the youth. In Canada and elsewhere, many educators are pushing for anti-racism education (see Thomas 1984; Lee 1985, 1994; Walcott 1990; Dei 1993). Those who have written specifically on the education of Black children have also called for a critical examination of what both African-centred knowledge and African-centred schools can do for the youth (see Henry 1992; Collins 1994; Farrell 1994; Dei 1995). In effect, these are not mutually exclusive educational philosophies. One call is for the incorporation of an African-centred knowledge into the mainstream curriculum as part of an effort to achieve inclusive schooling. The second call is for the establishment of African-centred schools to cater to those students who cannot adjust to the conventional school for a variety of reasons. For now, I will concentrate on the first approach since the latter is the subject for discussion in Chapter Six.

In terms of transforming the school curriculum through integrating African-centred knowledge and pedagogy, I share Asante's (1991) idea for the study of phenomena, grounded in the perspectives and epistemological constructs of all peoples of African descent. Like Hilliard (1992), Henry (1992), Ladson-Billings (1994), Lomotey (1990), C. Lee (1994) and Shujaa (1994), I see African-centred education as a state of mind that recognizes the pedagogic and communicative potential of African peoples' traditional and cultural knowledge base and social values of communal and humanitarian existence. As a theory of educational change, African-centred pedagogy explicitly locates the theorist and the practitioner at the centre of the analysis. It draws from the diverse historical and contemporary experiences and includes the appropriate centrality of Africa and African peoples as creators and producers of knowledge.

The notions of culture, power and pedagogy are fundamental to the conceptualization of African-centred knowledge. The relevance of culture in schooling and education processes goes beyond an interrogation of what culture means and how the term has become, for some, a powerful explanatory tool for understanding students' failure and/or academic underachievement (e.g., the culture deficit model). A critical examination of how culture is taken up in students' learning and educational experiences is needed (see Razack 1995b). Culture can significantly facilitate education by locating students' learning in appropriate cultural contexts. Culture has also become a site for students' resistance in schools (see Solomon 1992). In fact, as hooks (1988) points out, marginalized groups rely upon a unified identity to resist domination. Ibrahim (1994) also has recently shown how individual students take up identity, positioning themselves in pedagogical and communicative discourses and practices to exert their agency in schools. In such cases the ideology of a shared culture is central to articulations of (group) identity.[7]

There exists a wide body of relevant research and writing about pedagogy and culture in the North American context. In Canada and the United States, Henry's (1992, 1993a) and Ladson-Billings' (1994) respective works on Black teachers and classroom pedagogy articulate how the practical implications of curriculum inclusivity can be addressed at different levels, utilizing the cultural knowledge of parents, students and teachers. Educators are urged to tap the "cultural capital" (Bourdieu 1970) students bring from their communities to the school setting. Henry (1992: 175–83) cites the work of Ladson-Billings (1989) and many others to show how the educator can and should make a connection between students' school, home and broader cultural knowledges. Following Banks (1993: 7) "home culture" refers to the concepts, explanations and interpretations of society that students obtain from personal experiences in their homes, families and communities.Walcott's ongoing work also points to the importance of teachers using rap music and hip-hop culture, for example, as pedagogical tools in the schools. He points out that, through the validation and use of rap music and hip-hop culture, schools could be "unintelligible unto themselves . . . and education becomes a post-disciplinary space or a cultural studies venture" such that new forms of interpretation are possible (Walcott 1995: 143). Developing a pedagogy of the "home" and the "street" allows for the inculcation of specific cultural values, ideas, norms, social mores and culturally appropriate modes of behaviour and conduct in the processes of delivering education (see Zine 1995: 21).

"Culturally-relevant teaching" (Ladson-Billings and Henry 1990: 82) allows students to use their home culture as a basis upon which to critically interrogate "school knowledge." It subsequently renders the school a site of social and political struggle (Henry 1992: 183) that can be empowering for students and teachers as they collectively engage in social criticisms and a destabilization of the status quo. Students are able to question both what is passed on to them as valid knowledge, and the inherent contradictions of receiving an education that is not appropriately grounded in their lived experiences and cultural knowledge (see McLeod 1991: 206). Erickson (1987), in pointing out that cultural differences between students and teachers do in fact affect students' educational achievement, also stresses the political implications of understanding the oppositional cultures of Black and other minority students. He sees "culturally-responsive pedagogy" as one means of engaging in transformative teaching and learning that will equip students with the educational capital needed to deal with the contradictions between the norms and values privileged in the school and the harsh realities of students' "home" (off-school) experiences (Erickson 1987: 342; see also Banks 1993). Students' home and off-school cultures are part of their histories and lived experience; strategies of inclusive schooling should be able to draw on both the theoretical and practical aspects of such a body of knowledge.

Ladson-Billings' (1992) call for a pedagogy that empowers students intellectually, socially, emotionally and politically by using cultural referents to shape knowledge, skills and attitudes is significant. Such pedagogy moves beyond a superficial definition of culture which focuses on the "saris, samosas, and steel bands" (Donald and Rattansi 1992: 2) or the folk dances, foods and festive costumes. Instead, culture is seen as a dynamic force that is shaped and reshaped "through experiences generated in political and social struggles and through group interaction" (Benn 1995: 12). But, just as the critical anti-racism educator cannot unproblematically link race and culture, so must culture not be seen simplistically as a site of strength and knowledge when articulating the connections between culture and pedagogy. Educators who develop pedagogical practices that celebrate and validate students' multiple cultures and heritages are engaging in a transformative educational project which will destabilize and break down oppressive structures and barriers which have historically and continually served to exclude, marginalize and alienate minority youth in particular.

To discuss the specific connections and congruence between anti-racism education and Afrocentric education I highlight the basic ideas and principles of African-centred knowledge below.

Basic Principles of African-Centred Knowledge

By "African-centred knowledge" I am referring to the common-sense ideas and highly structured knowledge systems of African peoples about the everyday realities of living. These knowledges form part of the cultural heritages and histories of all African peoples, as do knowledge systems among other peoples. I refer specifically to the epistemic saliency of cultural traditions, values, belief systems and worldviews of society that are imparted to the younger generation by community elders. Such knowledge constitutes "African-informed epistemology" (Swartz 1992: 341). This way of knowing shapes a community's relationships with its environments. It is the product of the direct experience of nature and its relationship with the social world. It is essential for the survival of society. And, it is "indigenous" in the sense of resulting from long-term residence in a place.[8]

In contemporary contexts, using the term "indigenous" may set up a false dichotomy: indigenous and non-indigenous. This is avoidable if it is understood that the "past/traditional" and the "modern" are not frozen in time and space. The past continues to influence the present and vice versa. There is a continuity such that cultural values from past experiences help to shape the present. In its specific usage here, I share Muteshi's (1991) reasoning that the indigenous past offers a means of staking out a position as African which is outside of the identity that has been, and continues to be, constructed by Euro-Canadian/American ideology.

In traditional African societies certain social values were singled out for emphasis (e.g., social reward). Some of the major themes emphasized in various indigenous African ways of knowing were community membership, social responsibility, social cohesiveness and the commonality of all peoples. Such ideas and knowledges were expressed in local traditions, cultural beliefs, traditional songs, fables, proverbs, legends, myths and mythologies.

In developing the basic teachings of African-centred knowledge, it is important to acknowledge the ethnic and cultural diversity of African peoples. However, I share the sentiment of others (see Mazrui 1980; Gyeke 1987; Ayittey 1991) that beyond the fragmentation of culture along ethnic, religious, ideological, class and gender lines, lie some common themes.

It is also important to recognize that indigenous knowledge systems do contain sources of cultural disempowerment for certain groups in society, such as, for example, women and ethnic/cultural minorities. Hilliard (1992: 13) points out that no cultural tradition is immune to criticism. I am also aware that "tradition" has been used by the most powerful in society, when it is expedient, to perpetuate domination and oppression and to silence "other" voices. Furthermore, there are multiple forms and collective origins of indigenous knowledge. These principles are not unique to African cultures; rather, they are shared by other indigenous groups in varying forms and contexts. However, the importance of the common social values, particularly as they relate to anti-racism education, is the challenge they present to the assumptions of Western, hegemonic philosophies and epistemologies. Categories, individuation, despiritualization and, most importantly, individual ownership of knowledge are all refuted.

The following are what I consider to be twelve of the basic principles of African-centred knowledge. In developing these principles I have been influenced by the works of Wiredu (1980), Mbiti (1982), Hountondji (1983), Gyekye (1987), Mudimbe (1988), Okpewho (1992), Oladipo (1992) and Tedla (1995). These principles are interrelated and are not discussed in order of importance.

1. All knowledge is accumulated knowledge, based on observing and experiencing the social and natural worlds. There is no marketplace for ideas i.e., knowledge that can be bought or sold in the Eurocentric sense. This principle recognizes the link between knowledge and experience. It also takes the position that there is no sole authority on knowledge. Having cultural and political repositories of traditional knowledge in communities does not necessarily imply that the individual or group has exclusive ownership of, and control over, the process of knowledge production and dissemination.

2. We are all learners of the social and natural world. That social learning has to be personalized in order to develop the intuitive and analytical aspects of the human mind. In other words, every way of knowing is subjective and based in part on experiential knowledge. Such personal subjective identification with the learning processes makes it possible for the individual to be invested spiritually and emotionally in the cause of social change. It is particularly emphasized that the acquisition of knowledge is a process of interactions between the body, mind and the human spirit. The action of thought itself is a causal factor in social action.

3. All knowledge is socially and collectively created through the interactive

processes between individuals, groups and the natural world. This principle does not attribute knowledge acquisition simply to individual acumen, talent or to the limits of one's own senses. Knowledge comes from individual, family and communal interactions, as well as through the interactive processes with nature. The principle involves the collective activities of the social group, as well as natural and spiritual forces of the world (e.g., power of the ancestors and gods).

4. Humans are part of the natural world. We do not stand apart and neither are we above the natural world. This principle affirms that our basic humanness is a value system which speaks to the importance of relating to, rather than dominating, nature and the environment. This humanness stresses points of conciliation, rather than presenting the universe as a world to be studied and dominated.

5. To understand one's social reality is to have a holistic view of society. It is conceded the social, political and religious structures of society are connected to each other and that, for example, we cannot separate politics from economics, culture, religion, cosmology, family and kinship.

6. History and social change are processes which do not completely lie outside the purview and power of human agency. While the act of change itself is sacred, humans nevertheless can predict and cause social change with the blessing of the powers of the natural world (e.g., ancestral spirits).

7. Both our social and natural worlds are full of uncertainties. There is no certainty in any knowledge. Every way of knowing is clouded by some uncertainty about the social and natural worlds. Humans do not need to strive to explain away everything about their world.

8. Humans do not possess the Earth. It is argued that all living beings have borrowed the Earth from the ancestors, and that the living would incur the wrath of the ancestors if they destroyed nature in the process of satisfying societal and individual material needs.

9. The concept of the individual only makes sense in relation to the community of which he or she is part; the collective spirit is stronger than the individual mind. The uniqueness of the individual is recognized in terms of her or his personality, spiritual essence, talents and "destiny." However, it is argued that such individuality must be defined and placed in the wider social and political contexts (see Bray, Clarke and Stephens 1986; Semali and Stambach 1995).

10. To every individual or group right in society is married some fundamental responsibilities. The philosophical argument is that no one gets something for nothing and that one has to give back that which is received so that others may benefit.

11. Every life form exists in paired relationships (see Holmes 1995 for the Hawaiian example). The principle also recognizes that humans live in a continuous rather than a fixed, linear time frame. Thus, there are no such

fragmented categories in life (as in young/old, individual/communal, mind/body, personal/political and social/natural). To deal with these facts of life it is contended that humans need a non-dualistic mode of thought that balances all social and natural relationships. In other words, indigenous ways of knowing are not based on fragmented categories.

12. Knowledge and survival go hand in hand. In other words, we cannot separate theory from practice. The key to human survival is the ability of society to pass knowledge down through generations by cultural transmission and through teaching by example and practice (e.g., community work and action).

The challenge is for the anti-racism educator working in Euro-Canadian/American school contexts to harmonize and integrate these principles of African thought with European, First Nations, Asian and other systems of thought. There is some recognition among African peoples and other societies of the corrosive nature of the learning process and the fact that knowledge itself is created out of a series of socio-political arrangements and within certain contexts. Finding an appropriate fit between indigenous/African-centred knowledge and Euro-Canadian/American worldviews means doing away with all forms of hegemonic metaphors. African-centred education makes no distinction between indigenous and school forms of knowledge. It does not devalue the knowledge of community elders, parents and all those in traditional positions of authority. The view of African-centred education is that learning happens in a variety of social settings and that formal schooling and education outside school contexts can work together to meet the intellectual, cultural, social, philosophical, spiritual, emotional and material needs of the youth. Learning about such indigenous ways of knowing and relating to one another resists the totalizing logic of Eurocentrism (see McIsaac 1995). However, there are some risks involved in generalizing about the philosophical and sociological foundations of indigenous African knowledge.

Differences within Black/African communities have to be taken into account when espousing an African-centred pedagogy. As Hunter (1983) notes, although Afrocentricity has a target audience, the Afrocentric discourse cannot have one, and only one, meaning for all African peoples, irrespective of class, geographic location, ethnic and gender differences. Black and African peoples are a diverse group, with multiple and varying social identities that have to be recognized. Furthermore, as alluded to earlier, culture is not biologically determined and discourse about African culture(s) does not rule out people on the basis of perceived phenotypical differences. In espousing an African knowledge base, the educator also has to guard against what Lazreg (1990) sees as an attempt to wrestle certain features of indigenous life out of their contexts and insert them within a discourse that supports a political agenda. Muteshi (1991) cautions against reifying the "African cultural past" by constructing the past as if it is frozen in time and space. Thus, education rooted in the principles of African knowledge systems cannot seek to recapture a fossilized past. It must seek to recapture a past which holds valuable lessons for the present and the future.

The pursuit of an African-centred education presents some specific challenges for all educators. For example, can we talk about the need for an inclusive curriculum in Euro-Canadian/American schools and, in the same breath, highlight the importance of an African-centred curriculum? There is a seeming contradiction in speaking about a non-exclusionary Afrocentric pedagogy as this, like all pedagogies, is bound to be partial and exclusionary. How would the educator address the incongruity between the assertion of inclusive education (which addresses race, gender, class, sexual differences, religion, disability) and a focus on African-centred perspectives? What are the implications of an African-centred curriculum for the schooling and education of non-Black students?

As I argue elsewhere (Dei 1995), these are all legitimate questions that do not in any way negate the usefulness of African-centred knowledge in Euro-Canadian/American contexts. These questions serve to guide a critical discussion about the challenges of developing an inclusive school environment. Some current writings on African-centred education have moved beyond these questions to issues of implementation (see Shujaa 1994). There is also long-standing research evidence in the United States suggesting that an African-centred curriculum can improve upon the educational achievement of Black students (see Campbell and Wirtenberg 1980). However, more research is needed on the impact not only on Black students but on non-Black students as well. While Afrocentricity, for example, is a worldview adopted in opposition to the subjugation of non-White peoples by Eurocentrism, it is not an attempt to replace one form of hegemonic worldview by another (see Harris 1992: 306; Kugler 1995b). Knowledge of African indigenous cultural values, as with knowledge of other peoples, is important for the personal development and schooling of all students. A critical reading of the history of colonialism and neo-colonialism in Africa, and an acknowledgement of the achievements of peoples of African descent, both in their own right and in terms of human development, will be helpful to the progressive politics of educational and social change.

Curtis Banks argues that African epistemological constructs speak to people's sense of the "meaning, and functioning of the Universe and the natural context of their own existence [as well as] . . . values, principles, and standards of ethics and morality" (1992: 266). They are "established sets of ideas by which life is made understandable" by African peoples (Oliver 1986: 18). African-centred knowledge, like other forms of indigenous knowledge, recognizes the need to deeply root students' learning and education in a spiritual foundation, and provide the youth with a sense of individual and collective identity and responsibility to a larger/global citizenry.

These ideas, no doubt, have implications for Euro-Canadian/American education. The idea of community membership and social responsibility should be of importance to everyone. The pedagogic and communicative message is that, while individual rights are significant, schools must see the maintenance and performance of social responsibility as fundamentally important. These values and ideas should form the cornerstone of pedagogy in Euro-Canadian/American contexts. All pedagogues and school administrators have to recognize their mutual interdependence with other learners in the school setting. For the Afrocentric educator, an awareness of personal location, authority, experience and history is crucial to a successful teaching practice. Rather than claim authority in relation to text, knowledge or experience, the teacher must be willing to share power in the classroom, to know when to step outside the role of authority of knowledge, and to be able to engage students collectively in the cause of social change (see hooks 1994). The principles of African-centred knowledge teach us that knowledge is constructed in concert with others (see Tierney 1993b: 48 regarding a different context).

The notion of social responsibility introduced through schools to youth should advocate making the necessary interconnections between groups and individuals, and subordinating individual interests and wishes in favour of the common good. Educators should also make connections between the social and natural worlds to offer a form of holistic education. All knowledge must be shared. Knowledge must also be seen as the outcome of the interactive processes of the individual body, mind and soul and the wider social and political arrangements of society. And the false separation of the "home" and "school" must be broken as part of the wider task of constructing collective responsibilities. Admittedly, an uncritical endorsement of the notion of "community" is bound to reproduce relations of domination in society. As Khan (1995) points out, "community," as defined within a multicultural framework, is reduced to a liberal acknowledgement of difference without the recognition of power imbalances or the marginalization of the "other" in Euro-Canadian/American society.

Connecting Anti-Racism with African-Centred Knowledge

There is potential for utilizing Afrocentric ideas to buttress arguments for anti-racism education in the schools. In fact, the case for connecting anti-racism education and alternative forms of education, such as African-centred pedagogy, can be made along seven basic themes:

1.   Education in the Euro-Canadian/American context can never rid itself of an Eurocentric frame of reference. This is because most educators have been schooled in Eurocentric knowledge. Educators are likely to pass this on to their students. Nevertheless, what critical education and transformative learning through oppositional discourses like African-centred pedagogy can do is challenge Eurocentric knowledge as the only legitimate way of knowing about our world. It should understand that "all people can learn to centre in another experience [and] validate it . . . and there is no need to

'decentre' anyone in order to centre someone else . . . one only has to constantly and appropriately 'pivot the centre'" (Barkley Brown, cited in Caraway 1991: 192).

2. Alternative anti-racist forms of education like Afrocentric education are needed in the schools to help Black/African youths reinvent their Africanness within a diasporic context, and create a way of being and thinking that is congruent with positive African traditions and values (see Lee-Ferdinand 1994).

3. The success of anti-racism education in the schools will depend in large part on the ability of students to learn about the values, beliefs and traditions of their various community cultures, so as to strengthen their social, emotional and psychological well-being. Afrocentric education can particularly assist students of African descent to understand and affirm their home and community cultures and the interconnections with other cultures.

4. Conventional Western education has long defined non-European communities as ahistorical. Alternative anti-racism pedagogies, like African-centred knowledge, can be promoted to emphasize the rich and diverse historicities of the various constituents of the school body. Such knowledge would reflect power-sharing in the transformation of the curriculum as students who gain control over knowledge about their communities are empowered to challenge the status quo. The resulting curriculum would speak to and about the "experiences, histories, struggles, and victories [as well as] . . . voices, visions and perspectives" of marginalized groups (James Banks 1992: 33).

5. Conventional schools need anti-racism curricula that enhance alternative teaching practices by emphasizing "co-operation" rather than "competition" as the ultimate good in society. The teachings of African-centred knowledge emphasize the ideals of community and social responsibility. Even where current dictates of global markets/economies require competition, schools would teach how competition can be pursued in a more fair and equitable manner.

6. Conventional schools require alternative anti-racism pedagogies that emphasize moral and holistic education, and which teach students to associate themselves spiritually with the positive values of their cultures, languages and communities. African-centred pedagogy seeks to connect the individual student to a spiritual and moral foundation so that he or she can cultivate self-respect and respect for others, and recognize the importance of relating to one another in a non-divisive and non-exclusionary way. The Afrocentric emphasis on the spiritual aspect of teaching creates a safe environment in schools for all students to make connections between their material existence and a spiritual order of their choice.

7. The promotion of anti-racism education in the schools requires the retraining of teachers (by anti-racism workers), as well as the hiring of new teachers to reflect the diversity of our population. Some of the educators should

necessarily be Afrocentric, in the sense of undertaking a critical interrogation of Africa's past, culture and traditions to see what they have to offer the rest of humanity in general, and peoples of African descent in particular. For a more diversified teaching program to succeed, a more inclusive school environment must also be created for minority youth to arrive at effective learning outcomes, and to encourage them to pursue teaching as a profession.

Among the many challenges facing Euro-Canadian/American schooling is the partiality of what has come to be accepted as valid knowledge. The education system wittingly and unwittingly teaches about the cultural superiority of European peoples. African-centred education, as a legitimate strategy of anti-racism education, seeks to rupture such ethnocentric ideas. Ong (1988) has talked about the ethnocentrism inherent in the post-modernist "valorization of the individual." Conventional pedagogical practices appropriate the space for "valorizing the individual," especially through the ruthless individualism propagated by the mainstream school system. It cannot be denied that the emphasis on individuality makes it difficult to engage in collective ventures to question established structures and relations of domination since the power of human agency for the most part is located in the individual.

Critical educators have to be careful about extending notions of individualism to schooling settings occupied by students whose cultures are historically, politically, ideologically and spiritually collective and communitarian. One of the things the mainstream school system has continuously done is devalue the collective memories of minority students as members of a historically oppressed group. For example, an important factor why African cultures/communities survived slavery and colonialism was the recourse to their collective strength. The history of resistance is imbued with individual as well as collective endeavours. Within traditional African cultures, individuals are taught to link their objectives and survival to a wider collective. This calls for individuals to assume group responsibilities. The performance of civic duty is held in high esteem. Given the history of Black and African achievements in the diaspora, it could be argued that every contemporary individual success owes much to the struggles of Black forbearers. Schools deny this Black collective experience by negating race and its implications for schooling in very subtle ways (see Dei, Holmes, Mazzuca, McIsaac and Campbell 1995). When schools stress "individuality" the practice runs counter to the cultural and historical knowledge and memories, particularly when Blacks are continually stigmatized and subjected to differential (negative) treatment. African-centred education seeks to critically redefine the patriarchal structures and relations of schooling, and to make education politically and academically relevant to the aspirations and concerns of particularly (but not exclusively) Black/African-Canadian students.

In order for students to be empowered in their own learning, schools will have to address the imbalance of power in the production, distribution and dissemination of knowledge. This means promoting alternative non-hegemonic and oppositional discourses (such as Afrocentric, Asiacentric, Aboriginal-centric pedagogies) to challenge the hegemony of Eurocentricity. It means having teachers in the school system who will seek the appropriate centrality for each student in the classroom, and also rupture the established concepts, paradigms and content of the conventional school curriculum. The representation of diverse physical bodies in positions of influence in the schools should have some implications for the students' ability to identify with the school and for their interpretations of the use of power and authority.

The ultimate question is how schools and well-intentioned educators can realistically accomplish educational change, given the constraints imposed by the lack of budgetary and resource materials, as well as the dearth of teachers professionally adept in anti-racism skills. North America has historically witnessed protracted political struggles when it comes to educational change and reform. As pointed out earlier, in Canada local community groups have historically spearheaded political organizing for educational change to address questions of inclusive schooling. The US has also seen unending battles over curriculum and textbooks (see Cornbleth and Waugh 1993). Not infrequently, the issue of allocation of resources (financial, human and material) has been hotly contested when it comes to publicly funded educational institutions. There is a social and economic cost to every form of educational inequity. Therefore, measures to make schooling more inclusive must not be bogged down due to a lack of material resources. Some re-organization of priorities may be required in a climate of dwindling resources. While it is important that all stakeholders contribute to the cause of education, such involvement should be driven by a view of education as being for the public good.

On the specific question of resource materials, there is an abundance of literature dealing with issues of race, difference and alternative knowledges. Some schools are expanding and improving their library collections to include critical materials on these fields of study. Furthermore, the educational goal of retraining teachers to be anti-racist and inclusive can be accomplished through various aspects of the education system. Faculties of education in the universities and teacher-training colleges need to redouble their efforts to diversify their pool of candidates for teacher-training. A diverse teaching staff will bring different perspectives to issues. Post-secondary educational institutions can introduce courses on race, class and gender, and on how these intersect with schooling processes. They can also support the creation of centres for the pursuit of African-centred, Indigenous-centred and Asia-centred knowledge and education. Such post-secondary institutions could be at the forefront of critical integrative anti-racism studies that address questions of difference and identity in schooling and education. They could redouble their efforts to offer professional training and accredited courses for school teachers in the emerging fields of anti-racism and alternative knowledges.

Notes

1. For example, today many indigenous and local peoples are attempting to reclaim and reinvigorate their marginalized, and in some cases, lost voices and knowledge. Local peoples are challenging common-sense views about "international development." They are unpacking the institutional ideologies that tend to obscure and distort their social realities. They are asking for their voices to be heard and included in the designing of projects and programs that purportedly seek to "improve" their living conditions. A clear example of this can be seen in many Third World countries when university and college students, teachers, market women, trade unions and other professionals go out to demonstrate in protest of government policies; the very policies that have short-changed local peoples in the so-called economic development deals reached with the international financial bodies like the World Bank/IMF. Local peoples are protesting and waging daily struggles for transparency and accountability on the part of foreign and domestic decision-makers and power brokers in their communities. In Euro-American contexts there is an invisible but fierce struggle to negotiate the balance of existing power relations in the transmission and application of social knowledge. The conceptualization of development has become a terrain/ arena to challenge dominant, Eurocentric discourses. In fact, listening to grassroots voices and concerns in social research comprises a case of searching for inclusivity in the process and outcome of knowledge production.

2. See "Immigrants: A Label that Sticks for Life." *Toronto Star*, 27 June 1994, p. A17.

3. According to Professor Agnes Calliste of St. Francis Xavier University, the Cole Harbour conflict arose from a fist fight between Black and White students in Cole Harbour District High School. This led to the arrest of predominantly Black students and some working-class White students. Black community members in Nova Scotia saw racism as the root cause of the scuffle, while school authorities and government officials sought to play down racism.

4. Prior to September 1993, the Ontario public school system placed students entering Grade 9 into three different course levels, based on ability: the *basic* or *vocational* level, the *general* four-year level and the *advanced* level, which includes courses leading to university entrance. This is a process referred to as "streaming." In September 1993, the provincial government destreamed Grade 9 classes as part of the reform measures intended to address the school dropout rate.

5. I use "fading out" to denote the fact that dropping out is the final act of a series of school and off-school developments/experiences that culminate in students becoming engaged or disengaged in school (e.g., skipping classes, sitting in the back of class, hanging out in the hallway, "acting up.") These events reveal that students can be in school in body but absent in mind and soul and gradually "fade out" of the system.

6. It is true that not every community member would have the time, flexibility and confidence to walk in and engage in the created spaces and the process. But the creation of such spaces allows people to think of creative and alternative ways to make the best of an available opportunity. The existence of the space can allow parents to think of possibilities and recognize their roles and responsibilities to match criticisms with concrete action. Besides, there are many in the local communities who would have the time, flexibility and confidence to take up the space. Parents can work collectively to pull together individual resources and talents to ensure the best for their children.

7. What I mean here is that it is important for any form of education to be grounded in

a peoples' cultural knowledge and information base. I take culture in this context to mean "whole ways of life" and the totality of social practices of a people. Students learn better if they can easily relate to what is being taught. This means an identification with the social practices and meanings of schooling and education. This form of education requires using students' off-school and home cultures as a base for their learning in a way that is both critical and affirming of the positive (i.e., solution-oriented) aspects of culture. For example, can hip-hop culture be a powerful educational and pedagogic tool for some students? Can students teach about their off-school cultures and facilitate learning in the schools? Can education be relevantly contextualized in the historical and contemporary lived experiences of students? These are some of the questions I am asking.

8.   I want to stress that I am not putting forward a dichotomous perspective of African-centred versus Eurocentric worldviews. I am not claiming that African-centred ideas are distinct to African peoples. These ideas are applied to varying degrees and for varying intents and purposes in different societies. Here I am identifying the values that are privileged over other forms of knowing/values in differing ways among African peoples.

Chapter Six
African-Centred Schools in North America: Going Beyond the Polemic

This chapter examines the idea of the African-centred school as an alternative learning environment in North America. Rather than integrating African-centred knowledge with other centred knowledges to achieve multicentric, inclusive schooling, as discussed in Chapter Five, African-centred schools cater to those students for whom the mainstream school is not appropriate. These two educational approaches are not mutually exclusive. Both strategies challenge conventional Eurocentric schooling by introducing anti-racism pedagogy and curriculum. The idea is to respond to the challenges facing schooling and education in racially diverse communities with multiple, overlapping strategies. My academic and political project is to interrogate the social and cultural issues which repeatedly arise from the relations of social and cultural difference. The idea of the African-centred school is presented as a recommendation for educational action. It is discussed here as one of several possible focuses for alternative schooling. The discussion is contextualized in the exploration of issues relating to the critical theory of alternative education framed in praxis. This approach is fraught with some danger (e.g., an easy slippage into a political rhetoric). As an anonymous reviewer of an earlier paper I wrote on this topic remarked, there is some risk of overstating the obvious and understating the problems which make the obvious seem so reasonable and yet unacceptable.

The idea of African-centred schools is a matter of intense public discourse and political debate, at least in some segments of the Black/African community in North America. In the Province of Ontario, alternative schooling for target groups (such as Blacks, gays and lesbians) is a hot issue in some education and media circles. The establishment of African-centred schools is seen to have fundamental implications for minority youth education in North America. My discussion draws upon the specific case of Ontario and identifies the implications and relevance for the wider system in the Euro-Canadian/American school setting. My ideas focus on the secondary level of schooling.

African-Centred Schools in North America

The African-centred school is an alternative learning environment, created to promote academic and social achievement by dealing with the educational issues contributing to the alienation, isolation and disengagement of students of African descent, in particular, from the conventional school systems in North America. As with African-centred education, the African-centred school problematizes Euro-Canadian/American hegemonic desires for individual sameness and their effects on students' educational "success," in the Eurocentric sense of the term. The school promotes the centrality of Black/African experiences in social history and human/social development. It is recognized that there is both a structural *linkage* and *tension* between different worldviews. While there are some similarities within the differences that characterize human groups, knowledge production and social activity, there are also significant differences. These differences cannot be ignored in the delivery of education in the racially diverse, multi-ethnic countries in North America. We need to deal with our differences, rather than negate or dismiss them, in order to highlight our commonalities in the objective of education. This may entail the search for differing approaches to solve complex educational problems and concerns.

The idea of an African-centred school is not derived from a dichotomous understanding of the world (e.g., a Black/White duality or version of the world). Rather, an African-centred school espouses the idea that there are relevant indigenous African cultural values and epistemic constructs—such as the notions of community, traditions of mutuality, and social and communal bonding—that form the educational foundation on which to promote students' academic and social success. While the cultural values and ways of knowing are significantly different from dominant Western worldviews, the two approaches are not mutually exclusive. The perception of a dichotomy in social relations or, specifically, between indigenous and Western worldviews is, in fact, the result of the hegemonic desires of Eurocentricity. As argued earlier, Eurocentricity has devalued and negated the saliency of non-Western forms of knowledge and their relevance to education in North America. An African-centred school challenges and reconfigures the boundaries of Euro-Canadian/American cultural hegemony by centring the ideas and knowledges of non-Western peoples to broaden youth education in North America. This challenge also involves developing a sustained critique of the conventional role of public schools in North America as supporters of modern capital, as well as corporate and state interests.

Schools are not culturally and politically neutral terrains. Mainstream schools in North America have acculturation functions and roles. Like any form of schooling, the African-centred school is grounded in a political and philosophical base. The school challenges the traditional roles of schools in North America and affirms and normalizes Blackness and Africanness in the school setting (Ladson-Billings 1995). This does not mean that an African-centred school glorifies everything "African." The school seeks to develop a collective political consciousness for students. However, the African-centred school provides more than critical education. The school engages in an emancipatory educational approach by ensuring that the curriculum and pedagogical practices engaged by educators speak to all the various realities of African peoples in diasporic contexts.

In April 1995, I attended the annual meeting of the American Educational Research Association (AERA) in San Francisco. At a roundtable session dealing with African-centred schools, African-American educator Gloria Ladson-Billings poignantly asked whether we (as African educators) can function as advocates of such schools and still cast a critical gaze on the idea of an alternative form of schooling for the youth. This is both a dilemma and an important challenge. It means that those who advocate for African-centred schools should also be prepared to critically examine the notion's underlying assumptions in order to ensure the educational success of students. There must be room for dialogue; attempts at a closure of the debate (whether by those who are staunchly opposed to such schools or those who are in favour of the idea) must be resisted.

In Ontario, the concept of Black-focused schools (which are now appropriately called African-centred schools to correspond with the philosophical principles being based on African-centred knowledge) was first proposed by a multi-level government task force. In November 1992, the "African-Canadian Community Working Group" proposed, in a report titled *Towards a New Beginning*, that one predominantly Black junior high school should be set up in each of the six Metropolitan Toronto municipalities. The fifteen-member working group was appointed by the four levels of government—federal, provincial, City of Toronto, and Metro Toronto (Working Group 1992). The report suggested a five-year pilot scheme, establishing a Black-focused institution where Black history and culture would be taught. Such a school would have proportionately more Black/African-Canadian teachers and administrators on staff than in most "mainstream" public schools. The agenda would be to provide Black students with the choice of an alternative learning environment and to develop their sense of identity and belonging to a school. The hope was that, by teaching about Black/African-Canadian students' heritages, such a school would deal appropriately with the problems of isolation and frustration that many Black youths experience in society. The report recommends that such a school be set up on an experimental basis and that the students be kept together for at least three years. Students would come from a wide range of racial, ethnic, socio-economic and immigrant backgrounds.

The Ontario Royal Commission on Learning (RCOL), after an exhaustive study of the provincial school system, recently recommended that "school boards, academic authorities, faculties of education, and representatives of the Black community collaborate to establish demonstration schools" in jurisdictions where there are large numbers of Black students (RCOL 1994: 78). This call by the Royal Commission has added additional and interesting dimensions to the debate on alternative schools in Ontario. The idea of "demonstration schools" is a significant proposition that even the most ardent supporters of Black-focused schools cannot lightly dismiss. I say this notwithstanding the fact that the RCOL's idea of "demonstration schools" differs philosophically, ideologically and politically from the notion of an African-centred school. The "demonstration school" notion is still couched in the language of "inclusive schooling." The crucial point here, though, is that a "demonstration school," however conceptualized by RCOL, is necessary in the same way that a more drastic action to establish African-centred schools is and should be. Both ideas are conceived with the goal of securing the best for the youth.

Why the Need for African-Centred Schools?

Leake and Faltz, referencing the US context, argue that "there is a growing sense that our public schools have not only failed to address the persistent, pervasive, and disproportionate underachievement of Black students, but have perpetuated it" (1993: 371). This statement is not "school-bashing." It does not deny the fact that there are many devoted and inspiring teachers and administrators continually working hard to improve upon educational outcomes for all students. Schools should rightly take credit for students' successes. As a society, we should be able to celebrate the educational successes of our youth. But schools and society as a whole must also not shy away from accepting responsibility for the failures.

There are many reasons for advocating for African-centred schools. In fact, one only has to read a few of the countless research reports, academic studies and anecdotal comments on the education of Black youth in Euro-Canadian/American settings. There is mounting evidence showing that there are profound disparities between the constitutional rights of peoples of African descent, as free citizens with a right to fair and equitable learning outcomes, and the unfortunate educational realities of our children. Many African-Canadians likely share the important observation made by the RCOL that there is a "crisis among Black youth with respect to education and achievement" (1994: 93). It is true that many youth of African descent are succeeding at school. But these students share a deep sense of frustration and alienation. The fact that some students do well despite feelings of social marginality and masked frustrations should not give comfort to anyone. Their strategies should not be presented as logical pathways for other students to follow while structural elements causing students' social marginality remain unvoiced. Educational approaches to address youth concerns should not be narrowly presented as responses for those students who are "failing at school."

Black youth have been crying out for schools to be more inclusive. In my three-year research, which examined African-Canadian youth experiences in a select number of Ontario high schools,[1] many students spoke about the fact that they cannot say: "This is my school, I see myself here and I belong here." In my study, I found three primary concerns pervade student narratives about school experiences in Canadian contexts: differential treatment by race, the absence of Black/African-Canadian teachers and the absence of Black/African-Canadian history (defined as the totality of lived experience) in the classroom (see also Board of Education 1988; Brathwaite 1989; James 1990; Canadian Alliance of Black Educators 1992; Little 1992; Henry 1992, 1993b; Black Educators Working Group 1993). These concerns are pervasive to the extent that they emerge in response to seemingly unrelated questions or descriptions. Many students describe encounters with authority and power structures that are perceived not to work in their interest. Students describe struggles to construct self- and group-cultural identities in a school environment that does not adequately highlight their cultural presence, heritage and history in either the official or hidden school curriculum. They also describe attempts to excel in the face of unflattering teacher expectations. Although students are divided on the issue of whether to intensify parental involvement in the school, many students discuss their parents' assistance and sacrifices on their behalf. A number of students argue that they persevere because they want to be like their parent(s) and, conversely, describe the school environment as lacking role models.

When students are asked what aspects of their school system they would like to see changed, they talk about having more Black teachers. In response to questions about what having more Black teachers means to them, students tend to express a desire to see school environments with which they can identify. It is within this discussion, rather than in response to specific questions, that these students tend to make comments like "we want our own school." Such a clear articulation of the students' sense of disengagement from the present system and their expression of a proposed solution demands attention. How do we develop schools into "working communities" when some students feel alienated from the system? This is a very difficult problem. It demands that we come out with very creative solutions to the problem of youth alienation. Dismissing the problem as a matter of students' perceptions will not make it go away. In fact, we should be asking where do these students get these perceptions from. For many, if not all, what they perceive is their reality.

Research in the United States must be viewed in the context of differing histories and social realities, yet it provides insight into the issue of African-centred schools in Canada. There is a tendency for African-American achievement in predominantly African-American schools to surpass that of their peers in integrated schools (Leake and Faltz 1993). There is also some evidence that urban public schools (regardless of the school population) tend to reflect strong White middle-class biases in the curriculum and in teacher attitudes (Witherspoon 1987). Low teacher expectations, differential treatment and testing/placement by race are problematic for Black students in situations where teachers/administrators are White (see Morgan and McPartland 1981; Washington 1982; Preudhomme 1986; Smith 1989; North Carolina Advisory Committee to the U.S. Commission on Civil Rights 1991; McFadden 1992; International Institute for Advocacy for School Children 1993). Further, communities and researchers are proposing African-American Immersion schools as one solution to the problems of differential expectations, treatment and placement, a dearth of Black teachers/ role-models and an absence of African-American history and heritage in the schools (Leake and Faltz 1993).

In bringing some interesting perspectives to the debate on alternative schooling, Madhubuti points out that, in the United States, "Black schools along with Black churches led the modern fight for full educational and political equality . . . [and the] fight was never a battle to sit next to White children in a classroom" (1994: 3). It was a struggle for equal access and control over the valued goods and services of society so that all youth could equally seek to attain their life goals and ambitions. On the basis of a critical examination of the current educational achievement levels for Black students, it can be argued that the social integration of schools alone offers no guarantee for quality and equitable education. Having a diverse student population in itself does not guarantee social integration or the acceptance of each other. A cursory ethnographic observation of North American high schools shows a "segregation" of students in terms of students hanging out with their own racial groups in the hallways, cafeteria, etc. It is not simply a question of just encouraging the existence of a mixed student population but, more significantly, it is a matter of how knowledge is presented, how power is shared, how social rewards and benefits are distributed, and how the school seeks to centre students' lived and historical experiences in their learning. These are the key issues that enhance students' academic and social performance and ensure equitable outcomes for all students.

Writing in the US context, Ratteray (1990) argues that the education of African-American youth has been profoundly shaped by the problems of access to educational opportunities and to quality schooling. These problems are related to the broader question of educational inequity. There is still a disturbing disparity between Black and White students' academic achievement. Reasons for this inequity are rooted in the structural conditions of society and in the processes of schooling, rather than simply in the individual academic talents of students. Every mentally able child is naturally endowed with what it takes to receive education and to do well in school. The question is, to what extent do the school and off-school environments encourage or discourage this response? The idea of an African-centred school takes into account the historical and asymmetrical power relations that govern the lives of marginalized minority students in the mainstream school systems in North America.

The proponents of African-centred schools emphatically state that they are not calling for Black/African youth to be segregated from mainstream schools. But it is important to stress that the arguments and concerns of those who either favour setting up African-centred schools, or those who advocate Black youths remaining in a structurally transformed public school system, cannot easily be dismissed. The key question is, how best can concerns about minority education be addressed to meet the needs of *all* students? The idea of African-centred schools presents some challenges and questions for all advocates of an inclusive and equitable learning environment. For example, do Black youths need a Black community-owned-and-controlled school to address problems of school disengagement and academic success? How can it be ensured that the existence of African-centred schools would not distract from the legitimate pressures emanating from some Black and non-Black educators, students and community workers for mainstream schools to change their historical Eurocentric focus? How do we ensure that an African-centred school is not stigmatized in any manner by society?

These are significant questions. Responding to the educational needs and concerns of a diverse student body in Euro-Canadian/American contexts requires multiple and non-exclusionary educational strategies, as well as very radical alternatives which may not sit well with the dominant in society. Without a doubt, the call for African-centred schools is an outward manifestation of the larger problems facing Euro-Canadian/American school systems. The idea of such a school questions the fundamental objectives of public schooling, what they are supposed to teach and how, who graduates from the system and with what accreditation, and whose interests are reflected in the "deep" curriculum.

In a highly individualized, competitive society it is not surprising that notions of racial/ethnic collectivities, communal rights, group dominance or group subordination are hotly contested and staunchly denied. The emphasis on rights, individual merit and self-accomplishments is so pervasive that many refuse to acknowledge how systemic and structural barriers work to hinder individual and collective accomplishments in society. The ideology of individuals pulling themselves up by the bootstraps is so powerfully entrenched in public and political discourses, and the current lurch to the Right in North-American politics, only affirm the achievement ideology. Only a few question the axiom that labour participation or employment is key to social integration. In fact, witness the ultra-Right speaker of the US Congress, Newt Gingrich, recently making a case that the key to solving racial discrimination is employment and individual success and that no White American would mind if Black army general Colin Powell moved next door to them.

What Does an African-Centred School Entail?
An African-centred school is fundamentally governed by a set of shared principles rather than by who teaches, studies or works in the school. It is not that the latter are unimportant, but the principles govern who is part of or what goes on in the school (e.g., staff, student and faculty representation, as well as curriculum and pedagogical issues). In other words, questions about whether African-centred schools are for Black youth alone, or whether Black teachers alone can teach in such schools are not the key and immediate questions to be asked. An African-centred school cannot be defined purely as "same-race schools."[2] All who share in the basic philosophies of the school should find it a welcoming environment.[3]

The issue is not one of racial solidarity so much as cultural solidarity, that being an identification or affinity with shared cultural histories and values that transcend beyond skin colour and physical differences among peoples. For, as Gloria Ladson-Billings (1995) points out, racial identity does not guarantee academic success for African students. Of course, it may help in terms of developing students' ability to relate to the school. We cannot also dismiss the fact that so far non-Black teachers have not all had a tremendous amount of success in educating Black youth. In fact, given the political and economic climate and contexts in which African-centred schools are being recommended, it is important that such schools be open to all those who share the underlying cultural, ideological and philosophical principles of African-centred education. African-centred schools have relevance for non-Black students if it is understood that every student can learn to centre herself or himself in another experience and validate it without negating or devaluing her or his own experience.

African-centred schools are educational sites that seek to promote academic and social learning among the youth by centring and sustaining Black and African-Canadian cultures in the school system. Education in the school is culturally situated and aims at cultivating a sense of mutual interdependence among students, teachers, parents and the wider community. School, work and community are interwoven in the articulation of the experiences and social practices of all stakeholders in the school. Curriculum development and classroom instructional practice are informed by a holistic, integrated view of schooling and education which is based on certain philosophical values about the place of the individual in society. The school promotes education as a public good rather than simply for private interest, individual enrichment or self-improvement. However, while the school espouses the need for group empowerment and the upholding of a collective destiny, it does not negate individual self-worth and the right to self-determination by other social groups (see C. Lee 1994; Stinemetz 1995: 11).

An African-centred school offers an alternative approach to the delivery of education in society. Education in the conventional schools at times devalues any learning that takes place in the home and through the community. A part of the philosophical approach to education in African-centred schools is that learning and schooling happen in a variety of social and political settings. The formal school should therefore aim for some continuity between the learning that takes place in multiple sites (see Lightfoot 1980). In fact, Stinemetz also argues that education for Black children will only be successful when there is "continuity, trust, accountability, and responsibility shared between families, communities and school ... [and that] this type of relationship is difficult when there is a basic disregard for the relevance of culture [and power]" (1995: 4). A successful Black youth education is located within "African historical-cultural contexts" (Shujaa 1994: 28). Students' cultures, histories and personal knowledges are at the centre of the learning process in the African-centred school. Classroom instructional approaches extoll the virtues of community bonding, individual sharing, group mutuality and the matching of individual rights with social responsibility. The use of students' languages and dialects is encouraged as an effective pedagogical tool for academic success.

The idea of an African-centred school calls for imagining new forms of classroom teaching and pedagogy, new ways of fostering student-peer and student-teacher interactions, and developing new and alternative strategies for inclusiveness in the "deep" curriculum. Students also are educators in African-centred schools. For example, students teach about their out-of-school cultures (street/home cultures). Students are part of the team running the school. For instance, students sit on *all* school committees, including those that make major decisions affecting their school lives, staff hirings, retention and promotion, library acquisitions, curriculum changes and school budgetary allocations. Students should be legitimate partners and regularly participate in all equity discussions and decisions. They should regularly be allowed to review the academic work of teachers, as well as offer peer evaluations of themselves and their schools.

In the African-centred school, attention is paid to the spiritual and psychological aspects of teaching and the promotion of the social and emotional growth of students. The school places a high value on the teachings of parents, care-givers, community workers and elders in the holistic education of the youth. An African-centred school creates sites for parents, community elders and workers to come in to teach and learn from students and teachers. By instituting some form of adult education, students and teachers become part of the process of sharing knowledge with parents and community workers.[4] In effect, a truly African-centred education breaks the false separation between the school and the community.

An African-centred school is organized around communitarian principles and non-hierarchical structures. The school has a broad definition of students' success that includes the utilization of both social and academic measurements. For example, the performance of civic duty and social responsibility are significant factors in the evaluation of students' academic and social success. An African-centred school genuinely and unequivocally values the experiences of every member of the school. Education proceeds from an understanding that each individual stakeholder has something to offer and that the diverse viewpoints, experiences and perspectives of all strengthen the collective bond.

An important objective of the African-centred school is to address Black and African cultural omissions and negations in mainstream school texts and academic discourse. However, the issues go well beyond questions of culture to make links with questions of power. An African-centred school actively recognizes the connections between who is teaching, what is being taught and how, and how students are able relate to schools and the learning process. A philosophical assumption of the school is that students need to see teachers who look like them, share some aspects of their cultural and historical experiences, and appreciate diverse worldviews and perspectives. An African-centred school makes such identification possible through diverse representation among the teaching and administrative staff.

Admittedly, it is still uncertain how African-centred schools can deliver on the many expectations. The idea has not yet been tried out in Canada. Such schools should originate from, and be sustained by, local communities. There are historical examples of schools, developed in Nova Scotia and New Brunswick to meet the needs of Black youth, from which we can learn (see Castagna 1994). African-centred schools could be alternative schools which cater to those students who cannot adjust to conventional schools for a variety of reasons. Students may drop out of mainstream schools because of problems with teachers, fellow students, alienating curriculum or the absence of Black role models/ teachers. The question is not whether Black/African youth should continue to be mainstreamed or removed to ensure success. As African-Canadian educator, Vernon Farrell (1994), argues, the concepts of "alternative" and "choice" are significant in debates about African-centred schools. Students should have the right to be exposed to alternative learning environments and parents must also retain the element of choice as to which schools to send their children. It is not far-fetched to argue that, for students and parents who opt for an African-centred school, making the choice to go to the school may have significant implications in terms of enhancing students' attitudes in the school environment. Students' learning can be enhanced in an educational setting with which they can identify. Students who choose to leave mainstream schools to attend an African-centred school may develop some sense of identification with the school. For others, it may be a desire to challenge the current style of alternative forms of private schooling which cater to the upper middle-class. The desire is to secure counter-hegemonic alternatives that are not class-based and provide effective education for youth who feel disadvantaged due to the vestiges of social difference.

We cannot simply dismiss provocative and challenging ideas about alternative schools, particularly when these ideas have not been tried out. For those who say that the educational lives of the youth are so important that we cannot experiment with extreme ideas, a fair response is that many youth have for far too long faced enormous hurdles, leading to disengagement and fading out of school. These "fade-outs" have nothing to lose in trying an alternative learning environment. The idea of alternative-focused schools cannot be exchanged for a problematic understanding that time will correct concerns about minority youth education. We must get rid of the idea that time can solve educational and social problems. All that time does is pass us by. By now we should be learning from history. History must teach us something.

Equally significant, the debate about the effectiveness of such schools should not be conducted in terms of an either/or argument. We need to try multiple strategies to address issues of minority education. African-centred schools can be established alongside conventional schools and both forms of schooling can work together to address the mutual concerns of parents, teachers and community workers. It is a false and twisted argument that one cannot continue to pressure mainstream schools to be more inclusive at the same time as one is engaged in educational advocacy for African-centred schools. An African-centred school cannot meet the social and academic requirements of all students. By the same token, an African-centred paradigm cannot deny the existence of mainstream schools, and vice versa. Consequently, debate about the efficacy of the African-centred school should not be conducted through a dichotomous argument that would create a false confrontation between an African-centred school and an inclusive school. There remains a compelling need, within the Black community and the larger North American society, to devise multiple solutions for the complex issues of educating today's youth.

An African-centred school is a valid option that must be presented to parents and youth of African descent. The existence and success of African-centred schools can be a challenge to mainstream schools to live up to the ideals of genuine inclusion. The success of African-centred schools can put added pressure on the current school system to respond to the needs and concerns of a diverse student body. This is because most parents want their children to stay in inclusive schools. It is, therefore, not a contradiction to have *both* focused and inclusive schools. While all steps are purportedly being taken to make our schools inclusive, African-centred schools can be instituted for those parents who wish to send their children to these schools and those students who wish to go into such schools.

The argument that having African-centred schools simply means going back to the days of segregation is indeed problematic. There is a qualitative difference between "forced segregation" and "segregation by choice." Segregation involves more than physical space and location. The act of segregating a group always results from institutional and ideological aims. The institutional and ideological aims of those segregationists of the first half of this century were certainly meant to exclude others. These aims must be distinguished from those who want their children to be schooled in an environment free of oppressive bias in the 1990s. This distinction between forced segregation and segregation by choice (if indeed this is segregation at all) should mean something. It may offer useful and interesting lessons about the need for people to design and determine their own futures and to think out effective solutions to their own problems.

Similarly, the argument that an African-centred school would produce graduates whose credentials may be challenged and perhaps discriminated against in the search for employment needs critical examination. If one examines the United States context, there are influential African-Americans who went through predominantly Black colleges. If Black graduates are discriminated against in the job market, is it really because they went to African-centred schools? I would suggest that such discrimination is generally likely to be due to the structural and systemic barriers that racial minorities face, rather than to questions regarding their credentials.

At issue is whether there is something fundamental about African traditional values and philosophies that at some level can be distinguished from, and yet synthesized with, Euro-Canadian/American cultural values and worldviews. I believe that the values of group unity, mutuality, collective responsibility, community, and social and community bonding that were displayed many times in African and other indigenous cultural histories run counter to the current culture(s) of ruthlessly competitive and individualistic social formations. But an African-centred school does not see African communitarian principles in binary opposition to the American culture of individualism. The school aims at a responsible synthesis such that the place of the individual in the community and the community's relationship to the individual can be powerfully articulated.

Historically, issues of minority education in North America have moved uneasily from periods of assimilation policies, to integrative approaches which highlight tolerance of ethnic "cultures" and "minorities," to the multicultural education practices of recognizing diversity and difference, and finally to the current critical anti-racism education stance. As already argued, the anti-racism approach moves beyond the mere acknowledgement of diversity and difference in the schools, and calls for a rupturing and a radicalization of the notions of institutional power, education equity and democratic principles of North American society.

For many Black/African youth in North America, there is a paradox in the principles which inform Canadian/American democracy. There is a promise of equality which cannot be delivered by the state. We are at a critical juncture in our society as there is a conflict between our professed egalitarian values and the reality of sharp inequities in society. Mainstream educational institutions are sites for the cultural transmission of hegemonic ideologies and knowledges in the structuring of society along race/ethnic, gender, sexuality, ability and class lines. While it may be argued that state education systems have historically reinforced social inequities, the scope for social transformation through progressive education remains unclear. African-centred schools will have to embody structures that are radically different from those of contemporary mainstream schools if they are to have transformative and liberating potential.

The call for African-centred schools is part of the trajectory of expanding expectations of the public school system in a swiftly changing world. It is not a call to nurture "ethnic particularities" at the public's expense. It is also more than an attempt to command the direction of change for Black youths. It is part of the ongoing anti-racism struggle to empower youths to assume their legitimate positions in society and to fulfill corresponding responsibilities. Debates about the efficacy of such a school, therefore, have to be contextualized and understood as part of the historical struggle of subordinate groups to rupture Anglo/Euro-Canadian hegemony and the subsequent conformity of public schooling (see

Collins 1994). Black/African-Canadian parents and many educators want to stem the slippage of all youth in the education system. Black students need "free space" in an alternative school setting (as do other marginalized groups) where they can engage in political dialogue with educators, community workers and parents about the issues affecting them as participants in a White-dominated society.

It serves no useful purpose for anyone to simply dismiss these issues and concerns. It is significant to note that there are many minority groups who see African-centred schools through the eyes of the dominant society (see Farrell 1994). They are concerned about backlash, and an African-centred school would have to deal with that. Community support is vital in terms of sustaining African-centred schools. Community involvement and support are significant for the intellectual and emotional development of students and teachers.

An African-centred school brings up the question of "separate" or "independent" schools which currently tend to be private and more financially secure. It could be argued that African-Canadian parents are taxpayers and, therefore, have the same rights and responsibilities of mainstream school supporters. However, current events in Ontario, for example, provide some unpleasant memories. In the 1990s in Ontario many well-meaning governmental policies, from the Anti-Racism Secretariat and Employment Equity legislation to government funding of community programs, have disappeared in the wake of mainstream conservatism. For an African-centred school to take root, members of the community need to be assured that their funding sources are secure. Historically, state financial support has been tied to rights of control, accountability and governance. Hence, community control and monitoring of such a school is vital. The state will not relinquish its quest for control of the school if it provides all the funding. The African-Canadian community can carry out effective solutions to its "problems" if community members are willing to provide the required funding for the school. The knowledge that past separate schools have failed, due to inequities in state funding, should provide some significant lessons. The Black communities in Canada could take initiatives to secure local sources of funding for the school. For example, this entails exploring alternative funding sources from church groups and through local fundraising activities. As the members of the Working Group recommended, networks of individuals, businesses and community groups would work in partnership to secure the financial operation of the school. Furthermore the "partners" would form pedagogical alliances within the school, through co-operative work programs, voluntarism and skill development (Working Group 1992; 83–5).

It is important that the funding for such schools comes from the local communities themselves. Relying on outside funds would have implications for community control, as well as for the possibilities of alternative curriculum and pedagogical approaches. While I believe that the state has a responsibility to fund such schools, there are contradictions in terms of the objectives of an African-centred school and the reliance on the state for financial support. Historically, state financial support has been tied to rights of control, accountability and governance. Community control and monitoring of such a school is vital and the question is whether the state is willing to relinquish its quest for control as the one who pays the piper. These questions and contradictions will have to be resolved if these schools are to be successful. Furthermore, the success of such schools speaks volumes about our mainstream schools, and one cannot easily discount the extent of opposition to these alternative schools. In effect, an African-centred school must be prepared to deal with success and failure, and opposition.

There are other issues about African-centred schools that demand careful attention. For example, how do we prepare teachers for these schools? Finding the appropriate staff is a major challenge because an African-centred school should be staffed by teachers who are caring, willing to go the extra mile for students and are extremely dedicated to helping Black youth pursue their academic and social dreams. A history of demonstrated community involvement and strong commitment to the cause of anti-racism, equity and social justice are required, alongside teaching expertise, of those who are hired as teachers and staff in such a school.

At a theoretical level, an African-centred school also raises the question of how best can we, as a society, respond to the dictates of structural and cultural pluralism. How do we establish and sustain institutions and social service infrastructures that reflect the plurality of our society? There is a cost to equity, just as there is to social inequity. Leaving aside questions of who should fund educational institutions like African-centred schools, we may well have to accept a duplication of some services as a trade-off when responding to the legitimate concerns of subordinated groups in society.

The experiences of many Black youth in the public school system suggest an unending struggle to identify with an alienating system. An African-centred school could end up exacerbating their frustrations and further alienating them from society, unless particular attention is paid to defining the issues that act as significant barriers to students' educational success. Educators and school administrators must devise more appropriate ways than currently used in mainstream schools for measuring the outcome of such schools. Admittedly, in the Canadian educational setting, unlike the US (see Campbell and Wirtenberg 1980; Leake and Faltz 1993), there is little evidence linking Black teachers and a Black Studies-based curriculum to the academic progress of Black youth. This may be because opportunities do not exist for such curriculum to be offered and evaluated.

African-centred schools must provide appropriate cultural foundations for learners. Learning and educative practices must move African epistemological constructs of community renewal, integrity and social responsibility to the centre of meaningful pedagogical dialogue that includes students, teachers, administrators and the wider community (see Asante 1991; Watkins 1993: 331; Dei 1994c). But there should always be room in the schools' pedagogical practices and curriculum development for other non-hegemonic ways of knowing. At a more general level, the curriculum for an African-centred school must promote democratic learning, propagate ideas of common schooling, encourage emancipatory and liberatory thinking and engender genuine social transformation.

The challenge is to move beyond the polemics of both advocacy and critique to concrete action. This means ensuring that African-centred schools are not stereotyped and isolated, but instead are given all the necessary emotional, material and other logistical backing to achieve what these schools are intended to accomplish for Black and other youth. On the basis of our understanding of the fundamental principles of African-centred schools, our individual and collective energies should be devoted to the implementation of such schools at different levels in the North American education system.

Notes

1. Since early 1992, with the assistance of graduate students from the Ontario Institute for Studies in Education/University of Toronto, I have conducted a research project examining Black/African-Canadian students' experiences in the Ontario public school system. In one phase this project solicited individual and group responses from over two hundred students to such questions as: What do you like/dislike about school; why do you think some students drop out; and why do others stay on to complete their education? We asked students how the dynamics of social difference (race/ethnicity, class, gender) affect their schooling experiences and what changes they want to see effected in the school system. In the schools, students were randomly selected to provide a representation of male and female students from general and advanced level programs, and to include students in Grades 10 and 12. In subsequent phases of our project, we talked to teachers, guidance counsellors and parents, in part to cross-reference some of the students' narratives.

2. It should be noted that non-Black students can learn in an African-centred school as much as Black students. While a large segment of the school may be of Black/African heritage, the school will have non-Black students, teachers and administrative staff. It is not convincing enough to argue that Black students need Black role models or Black curriculum in the schools. Non-Black students also need to see Black role models (male and female) to mitigate social racism and the negative evaluation of difference.

3. While these characteristics are still at the ideas level, there are some relevant examples elsewhere. Although the Black population in Canada is a fraction of the group in the United States and has a unique history, projects in the United States offer some important lessons about the nature of African-centred schools. In Chicago, Washington and Detroit, Black educators maintain the efficacy of Black schools, as well as assert that the pragmatic goals of socio-cultural and skills development should remain central, within more idealistic goals such as intra-racial harmony (Kilson 1994: 17–18). Nonetheless, Canadian initiatives for Black schools may learn from the peculiarities of different social settings. In particular, Canadian educators and administrators may learn to incorporate aspects of the historic successes of predominantly Black educational institutions such as Howard University, Tuskegee

University and Spellman College. For example, in the 1980s while Black colleges only attracted 19 percent of Black students, they granted degrees to 33 percent of Black graduates (Martin 1984: 126).

4. As an example of adult education, parents may come into the school to share ideas with the students and learn about their off-school (street) cultures. Parents can also receive some help in basic literacy and science through the help of teachers, students and other community workers. Parents can upgrade their knowledge on current social and political affairs, as well as learn more about their histories and cultures. The entire process of parents sharing knowledge about community issues and social politics can be a powerful medium of adult education.

Chapter Seven
Anti-Racism and its Implications for Future Educational Practice

I set out in this book to discuss anti-racism education and its implications for alternative schooling and education in North American contexts. I have argued that anti-racism is an academic and political project to question and address racism and other forms of social oppression. I have pointed out that race is an important conceptual category on the basis of which power, prestige and privilege are organized, regulated, distributed and rendered meaningful in contemporary society. At the same time, anti-racism education cannot allow the category of race to eclipse other forms of social inequities or the myriad forms of oppressions.

Going Beyond Education
In this final chapter, I wish to connect anti-racism education in the schools with anti-racism political organizing in off-school settings. I take a broader view of the application of anti-racism and the definition of education. I revisit current concerns in the anti-racism praxis and posit some future challenges facing educators and social activists as we collectively work for fair and just communities. I explore some questions: What does it mean to engage in anti-racism politics of change? What are the implications of anti-racism politics of educational change and social transformation? Are there practical considerations which are more than tangential to the anti-racism project? Is it possible to engage in anti-racism educational change of the "deep" curriculum of schools when the very existence of the education system is dependent on a conservative social order? In other words, how do we develop a commitment to race and equity issues in a period of a remarkable lurch to the Right, a climate of fiscal conservatism and a strong backlash against, and scapegoating of, racial minorities and "immigrants"? Can the anti-racism project develop strategies to counteract the emerging hostility to race and anti-racism issues in schools and in the wider society?

These are difficult questions precisely because of what anti-racism stands for. As discussed earlier, anti-racism is a challenge to the status quo. This discourse is a voice displeased with the current social order and the problematic

122

practice of the most powerful in society aspiring to design the futures of the subordinated. Anti-racism is about the search for just political communities and an individually affirming social order. Anti-racism education seeks to build democratic communities in which individual rights to political representation and participation are appropriately placed in a broader context of communal interests and solidarities (see Eyoh 1995: 50, writing in a different context). Anti-racism is a challenge to colonialist discourses and practices in schools, workplaces and other organizational settings that create racial and cultural "others" by negatively evaluating difference. Anti-racism discourse questions the organization and transformation of non-European spheres and spaces into "fundamentally European constructs" (see Mudimbe 1988, writing in another context). Anti-racism questions the "virtual submissive silence" on the part of the educator in the face of gross racial, gender and class inequities. It is contended by anti-racism activists that those who continually live with the scourge of racism, and experience other forms of social oppression, need to redouble their efforts to sustain social movements rather than dissipate their energies in the construction of hierarchies of pain.

Anti-racism education also moves beyond the liberal commitment to "equal" access to education and individual freedoms and rights, to redressing collective rights and social injustice. While liberal discourse about the nature of society emphasizes individual rights and equality, there is no corresponding emphasis on collective responsibilities of citizens, the nation state and global community that will ensure that everyone has access to the valued goods, resources and tools needed to function effectively as members of society. We need to problematize the lack of freedom and choice experienced by a majority of people globally. Anti-racism takes up group concerns (rights and responsibilities) rather than repudiating them in favour of individualistic interests. Anti-racism defines citizenship in terms of rights and responsibilities of individuals and the cultural collective, that being all those who participate in a defined shared culture such as the nation state, local community and so forth.

One of the collective responsibilities of anti-racism activists is the engagement in political action to address questions of social inequality. The struggle for justice and equity is not simply a question of quantitative and qualitative differences in responsibilities. Responsibilities require a commitment, will and ability to carry through what is expected. We cannot simply dispense with responsibility because it is hard to achieve. While those who wield power have a responsibility to use their power to address injustice and domination, those who are subordinated have a duty to resist their domination and to demand that responsibilities be fulfilled. As Elias (1978) points out, dominant social actors can only reproduce their power as long as they are successful in binding those who depend on them to their cause. Thus, the political act of resistance is cardinal to the anti-racism cause.

For many racial minorities in Euro-Canadian/American schools, there is a persistent struggle to counter the hegemonic discourse of Eurocentrism. We are engaged in a political and academic task to produce, interrogate, validate and disseminate alternative and sometimes oppositional forms of knowledge. We are continually voicing resistance to the dominant culture. A call to avoid a dogmatic approach to every form of education is tantamount to a call to resist attempts at academic closure and academic domination. I am particularly concerned about academic debates dealing with meritocracy, individual achievement and academic freedom.

For example, the notion of "merit" is continually employed to diffuse calls to address equity issues in employment. It is as if the call for equity in hiring seeks to ignore the requisite qualifications that applicants must bring to a particular job situation. The fact that what has traditionally passed as "merit" in many cases is subjectively and socially constructed is conveniently denied. Similarly, when attention is drawn to structural processes and barriers that limit the life chances of racial and ethnic minorities in very racialized societies, one hears the opposing critique of "when will individuals begin to take responsibility for their own failures in life." There is a pervasive ideology of individual achievement that attributes conventional definitions of success in life solely to individual efforts and talents. Everyone can succeed in life if he or she works hard. Consequently the lack of conventional success is viewed as being due to an individual failing without any attempt to critically examine and work to remove structural barriers that may impinge on individual success. Within schools, colleges and universities there are many scholars who will staunchly defend academic freedom. The problem is not with academic freedom per se, but with its unqualified defence which includes the right to offend in the name of the pursuit of knowledge. Academic freedom cannot exist in a vacuum and out of a social and political context. As educators and researchers, we should be accountable to the communities we serve.

A source of disquiet is that there are no parallel discussions about definitions of merit, who defines merit, how and why, and how the recourse to individual responsibility masks the structural barriers many youth encounter in their schooling and in society. There are also no corresponding initiatives to tie academic freedom to academic responsibility. In engaging in this academic and social critique, it is not always easy to convince school administrators and educators that, with few exceptions, when educational criticisms are levelled, they are against the school system itself rather than at individual well-meaning teachers and administrators.

Anti-racism educational praxis calls for a collective politics to challenge all forms of domination. Anti-racism challenges all justifications for subordination and oppressive action. Political organizing for educational change and social transformation requires the collection, reflection and inflection of all encapsulated narratives about the practices of subordination, marginalization and exclusion in society and its institutional setting. In specific reference to the school system, engaging anti-racism means that educators make a commitment to listen to and act on minority students' voices and experiences. Educators challenge the processes that reproduce the normalcy or normativity of whiteness in their schools. Differences within student populations are noted in the pursuit of educational change. There is an awareness and critical exploration of how these differences emerge in the myriad contentions and manifestations of students' daily and educational experiences. The historical success of the school system in erasing students' collective and historical memories, as well as their experiences of being marginalized in a racialized, gendered and classed society, is not left uninterrupted. Anti-racism educational practices assist the youth to deal with the contradictions of a changing society and, particularly, the paradox of conflicting social and moral values.

The discussion so far has argued for positioning anti-racism at the centre of educational practice in North America. This is primarily because race is at the centre of Euro-Canadian/American social and political relations. Inequalities constructed by skin colour or race are not so easily transcended. In fact, as Fumia argues, there is a difference between those who can transcend their ethnicity through social integration and assimilation and those who "remain disadvantaged because of their race" (1995: 10; see also Walcott 1990).[1] We do not live in deracialized contexts. Even the idea of deracializing social policy can have unintended racist consequences (e.g., the push for Anglo-conformity).

It serves no useful purpose to adopt essentialist interpretations of the nature of social relations. A clear understanding of the dynamics of social difference provides a broader perspective on the dialectic between social and political structures, history and culture. Gilroy (1992) rightly called for moving beyond seeing race simply in terms of culture and identity, to the larger issues of politics and history. Racism is just one aspect of social oppression and the struggle for social justice transcends the "desire to do away with racism" (Gilroy 1992: 50). Gilroy, in this particular essay, goes on to stress that anti-racism workers cannot deal with racism while "leaving the basic structures and relations of society essentially unchanged" (1992: 52). I could not agree more. All the same, I would like to stress some related points.

Anti-racism politics must start from wherever we are at. We must engage in an educational and transformative practice, linking a politicized view of culture and identity at local levels with the broader structural objectives of global political economic transformation. Starting from where one is at means stressing the relevance of daily personal and collective experiences and their relations to current questions of culture and identity. This is what I term "grounded politics." I believe it is from the local level that we should move to connect the history and politics of broader structural concerns. In other words, with an understanding of a politicized notion of culture and identity, we organize locally to transcend local, regional and national boundaries and make our connections with global political economic issues.

We also cannot afford to reduce anti-racism to a struggle against global capitalism, even when dealing with racism means rupturing global economic and political structures and relations of domination. The issues of anti-racism extend beyond particular socio-economic formations. I agree that the anti-racism struggle should deal with the depoliticization of the concept and meaning of race. The shift from political definitions of race to a "narcissistic celebration of culture and identity" is indeed problematic (Gilroy 1992: 56). An overemphasis on culture and identity can easily slip into ethnic particularism, cultural reductionism and relativism and the perception of culture(s) as homogenous, insular and fixed. This slippage can obscure and, at the same time underscore, the dangers of engaging in a particularistic intellectual practice devoid of a global consciousness (see Moghissi 1995). I am referring here to a narrowly defined community politics for change which focuses on, for example, racial or class oppression in North America but fails to see their international dimensions. This is a failure to see how such oppressions can be, and indeed are, multifaceted and connected to the subordination and marginalization of the so-called developing world in the global politics of international finance capital, as well as the appropriation of wealth and resources of the South by the Northern World. The failure to see these connections makes it difficult to join political struggles to oppose oppressive forces that reproduce Euro-Canadian/American capital hegemony throughout the world.

Moving Beyond a Self-Referential Politics

A key consideration in the pursuit of anti-racism political organizing for social change is theorizing the personal and the political. A theoretical understanding of the personal is, in fact, a prerequisite for effective political action. Understanding the trajectories of individual and group experiences may point to significant lessons about alternative forms of social and political resistance to a myriad of oppressive human conditions. It is necessary for anti-racism workers to critically theorize both individual and collective historical and contemporary experiences in order for them to provide a methodology of social change (see Pierson 1991, in other contexts; Scott 1991; Butler and Scott 1992). Theorizing the personal and the collective starts with a critical examination of voice and experience. The voice that claims authority based on experience must be problematized, without necessarily denying individual agency. Self-criticism is crucial to anti-racism politics. As Scott (1992) argues, experience should not be a source of truth or the "origin of knowledge." Experience cannot be taken for granted. While we may seek to understand experience and practice as a contextual basis of knowledge and political action it must be noted that experience itself requires an explanation.

hooks (1994) elaborates on the importance of personal experience and how the telling of such experience can help "transgress" the boundaries of intellectual exploitation, appropriation and misrepresentation in education. Personal experience by itself is not enough to provide a complete account of social oppression. There are problems in claiming an "authority of experience" without recognizing how power relations shape the process of knowledge creation or construction. Personal experiences are lived through social relations of power.

Ahmad (1995) also cautions against the tendency to see human culture as "so discrete and self-referential, so autonomous in its own authority . . . [and] to privilege self-representation over all other kinds of representation and to treat self-representation as a moment of absolute authority" (1995: 16). No culture is insulated from events around it. A political understanding of culture in culturalist discourses can enhance anti-racism knowledge production. Borg (1995), borrowing from Gramscian thought, sees culture as a field of struggle in which the processes of producing, legitimizing and circulating particular forms of knowledge and experience are central sources of conflict. A politicized approach to culture and cultural differences allows for the interrogation of power relations embedded in the use of culture. Culture is seen as an embodiment of knowledge. It is not created out of a political vacuum. In a given society, as McLaren (1989) points out, there is a complex combination of dominant and subordinate cultures. Of particular interest to anti-racism praxis is the understanding of how the dominant culture comprises the ideologies, social practices and structures that affirm the central values, interests and concerns of those who control the material and symbolic wealth in society (McLaren 1989). This is the dynamic connection between social power and culture.

While anti-racism workers need to be critical of how individual and collective experiences are taken up in discursive and political practices, it is also important to underscore the fact that theorizing experience does not mean privileging all experiences and viewpoints. Self-criticism guards against the relativism which upholds the epistemic saliency of all viewpoints. The question to ask is: Where does plurality of voice lead to in the politics of social change? We may need to highlight subjugated viewpoints of non-dominant groups in society in discussions about social oppression.

An anti-racism project of social change allows social theory and theoretical abstractions to speak to the actual lived realities and conditions of those who are oppressed. As critical educators, our theories and academic scholarship have to be accountable (see Moghissi 1995) and speak to the materiality of human existence. For the anti-racism worker, a distinction between theory and politics can only be problematic. Theory and political practice are inseparable. Theory is about knowledge production while practice is about "practical politics." Rather than reify theory, the anti-racism worker must ground theory in actual political practice. Social justice activism is more than theorizing about change. It is about engaging in political practice informed by theory of social change, at the same time as the theory itself is refined by political practice. This is anti-racism praxis.

Within the public education system, one subtle way to resist oppositional discourses is to claim that there is no theory behind the counter-hegemonic discourse. There is a reification of theory which negates the idea that people live theory every day of their lives. Anti-racism teaching cannot be separated from anti-racism political activity. It is the political action aspect that makes anti-racism education activist education. The anti-racism educator's role is not simply to learn or discuss race and racism issues, but to challenge injustice by rejecting existing social relations of domination and oppression. In a racialized, classed and gendered society, counter-hegemonic education cannot be anything but anti-racist, anti-sexist and anti-classist. The educator's involvement in local community political activism for social change only helps strengthen educational and discursive practices in schools, workplaces and other educational settings.

A new critical approach to anti-racism praxis must be able to deal with the alternative and new ways in which racisms have emerged. An emerging concern of anti-racism praxis is how the discourse of difference, for example, is constructed and used in very political ways in education to divide social groups and individuals in society. Social difference is not just produced and reproduced. An a priori existence of difference is assumed and negatively acted upon. A new critical approach to anti-racism questions a politics of difference that fails to recognize power dynamics in society.

The Foucaultian concept of power and its relationship to knowledge has significant implications for anti-racism politics (see Foucault 1980). Knowledge can be understood in relation to one's subject location and interest. Anti-racism is about knowledge production, interrogation and use and the relationship with social power. The political project of anti-racism is to destabilize conventional knowledge and the modes of producing, questioning and disseminating knowledge and "stable authority" (Britzman 1995). This practice is bound to create dissonance in the stable minds of those who benefit from the status quo. If we agree that all social relations are power relations, then a politics of difference and identity must acknowledge the multifaceted dimensions of social power. In the context of anti-racism praxis, power works at two levels: at the level of intra-group dynamics (e.g., intra-group racisms) and at the macro-level of inter-group relations (e.g., majority-minority/Black-White relations).

There is a new populist politics that scapegoats "difference" and racializes "others." Our earlier discussions touched on new culturalist forms of racisms that do not rely on perceived phenotypical differences among people. Today we can speak of race without mentioning the word (Gilroy 1992: 53). The coded language which refers to "welfare mothers," "pushy immigrants" and "hangers-on" has become the popular refrain for those whose racialized discourses have the intent of blaming and punishing people. Racial meanings are easily inferred from powerfully coded words, as well as from the emerging definitions of citizenship and nationhood (see Henry, Tator, Mattis and Rees 1995). The use of language to convey differential treatment is a historic practice. However, in the current context, it has assumed new, powerful meanings in terms of both the subtle use of language and also the meanings attached to people who speak differently.

Apart from anti-Black, anti-Asian and anti-immigrant racisms, there have emerged different and complex processes of racialization. These utilize powerful ideological and political practices to identify particular populations by making reference to perceived biological and cultural unity. These populations are thought about and spoken about in racialized terms, using language, biology and religious definitions (see Reed 1994). One can point to the rise of neo-Nazism and fascism, and the public discourse and treatment of Muslims in Europe and North America as examples.

The consequences of the new culturalist and depoliticized approaches to race are manifold. The new forms of racialized discourses appear in subtle forms to reproduce and sustain hegemonic ideologies. These new forms make it easy for people to openly express racialized hostility without admitting that their actions are profoundly discriminatory. They also make it more difficult to organize against structural racism. In fact, Goldberg's (1993) reference to "consumer-directed discrimination" is in many ways connected to the power of an emerging populist politics of race-baiting.[2] It is not just that race policies today are driven by public opinion. There is open refusal to even explore the possibilities of a new society which could be pursued were we to feature anti-racism work and analyses more seriously in everyday social practices in schools, workplaces and other organizational settings. Let me provide a more direct example, using the quest for minority representation in universities as an illustration. The rhetoric of "equity in hiring" conflicts with entrenched, powerful interests protective of the status quo: the clientele, courses and programs that "have to be taught." These interests act as a stumbling block, preventing a rethinking of the conventional ways of teaching courses or disciplines. The case is made for protecting courses already on the books because "students want them." Conversely, there is no serious consideration of how a different audience would be attracted to universities were educators to feature anti-racism work and analysis more prominently in the design of courses and in the engagement of educational equity practices (see Rockhill 1995).

The Resistance to Anti-Racism

The social agenda for anti-racism and equity in the schools and other organizational settings is threatened, given the recent radical electoral shift to the xenophobic Right as represented in the 1994 congressional elections in the US and the victory of the Conservative governments in Alberta and Ontario. The "myth of tolerance" is exposed in political debates and public discourses that use individual "underachievement and indiscipline," as well as cultural differences, to explain social inequality and economic disadvantage. Both in public and academic discourses on race relations, one can hardly miss the false sense of cultural, moral and intellectual superiority held by some members of the dominant group.

The recent successful swing in the political fortunes of conservative forces is emblematic of the fear that most Whites have about losing their hegemony.

Conservatives appeal to mainstream White male anxieties about employment equity/affirmative action. Poorly concealed racist discourses on the fringe of the New Right movement and White supremacist groups have appealed to the sensibilities of many unsuspecting youths. In Canada, one only needs to witness the infiltration of Heritage Front members in some high schools in the early 1990s. Slogans like "angry White male" are commonly uttered as if they are non-threatening to minority populations. A similar slogan, like "angry Black male," would elicit outright public revulsion. In the schools, the era of fiscal restraint provides a convenient excuse for administrators to shed anti-racism initiatives. In the face of these constraints and conditions, the push for anti-racism change is branded as a political agenda of "special-interest groups." To say that "anti-racism is special-interest education" denies that everything we do is political, interest-bound and value-laden.

If anti-racism has become a corrective educational practice to some, it is because social relations and practices of domination have for far too long been presented as the "normal" and "fair" way of doing things. It is this sense of "normality" and "fairness" that anti-racism challenges, starting with the schools. There is open resistance to anti-racism and there are powerful interests to ensure the invisibility of this discourse in most institutional settings. To refuse to promote anti-racism is to engage in the politics of negation. Blinded by racist myopia, a few individuals are revisiting the discourses of colonial racism and propagating hate and resentment.

But the resistance to genuine social transformation takes many forms, the least common of which is co-optation. Today, even some organizations with good intentions have found it expedient to shape their take on anti-racism to serve corporate material interests. This can be seen in fledgling corporate and industrial capital designs to maximize profit by engaging in anti-racism initiatives. The commodification of anti-racism is very apparent as big business corporations jump on the bandwagon to promote a rhetoric of "equity and diversity." These developments are driven more by the specific and parochial interests of capital than any unshakable commitment to the cause of social justice. Economic and material interests, rather than concerns for equity and fairness, shape their strategies for change. Corporate discourse on anti-racism and equity is laced with political and economic considerations of population changes in North America which indicate that businesses stand to gain from having diverse staff. A new thinking relates a school's success to corporate economic and material interests. Furthermore, a number of individuals, acting as anti-racism consultants, are profiting from their engagement in anti-racism and organizational change issues. The problem is that many of these consultants have not demonstrated any commitment to the local communities on whose backs these riches are made. There is no community service offered and hardly any resources are devoted to the local communities.

In Canada, the state's position on anti-racism has so far been limited and not intended to disturb the status quo; it is a constraining response to community political organizing for real change to deal with equity and power-sharing. The social construction of race, as Train (1995) argues, serves to divide and position people differently according to socially constructed differences. The state reproduces its hegemony through the political construction of difference. For example, state-supported structures and Euro-Canadian culture render racial minorities and their experiences invisible through constant referencing in the image of the "other." As Walcott (1995) points out, we see this political act in the referencing of the United States when race issues arise in Canada.[3] Similarly, the "politics of funding" also reveals how the state selects its spokespersons and targets specific groups within the various ethnic communities for legitimation and for multicultural funding purposes. Notwithstanding the current changes being made, state funding for instructional materials, curricula development and reform by and large serves to reinforce Euro-Canadian dominance by regulating the processes of knowledge production, validation and dissemination.

Responses to Resistance

To deal with this subtle "resistance" to genuine change, there has to be a strategy of political and educational reclamation of anti-racism to ensure that anti-racism praxis serves local community needs and concerns for social justice, equity and power-sharing. The future of anti-racism may lie in the power of civil society to deliver justice and equity. But the local community's capacity for autonomous self-organizing for change (Gilroy 1992: 60) can co-exist with state policy initiatives for change. These strategies are not mutually exclusive. The truth is that the state remains a powerful, albeit a suspect, ally in the anti-racism struggle. The state propensity and capacity to marginalize race politics in the broader social and political ordering of society is phenomenal. Yet the state is a site of struggle where minorities and the oppressed can and do negotiate their interests.

Local community initiatives for anti-racism change will have to contend with state interests in containment. Anti-racism cannot be held as a political tranquilizer that obscures the sharp disparities in material wealth between social groups which contribute to reproducing the existing social order. The tools needed for a reclamation of anti-racism from state and corporate capital's interests include the development of a powerful language and voice by local communities. A language of anti-oppression is necessary to carry the political message for social change.

As already alluded to, anti-racism praxis seeks to create new communities for political action. The question is, how does one acquire the "language of reclamation" of anti-racism to engage in community/grassroots-level political organizing for change? My argument is that in order to acquire this language, anti-racism workers will need a grounded knowledge of the multiplicity of social oppressions, as well as an appreciation of the saliency of certain forms of oppression.

Edward Said (1993: 336) and many others have remarked that no one today is purely one thing (see Gilroy 1992, 1993a, b; Bhabha 1994). In fact, no one has *ever* been purely one thing. Social oppression impacts upon our lives in diverse ways given our multiple identifications and subject positions. Because of their diverse forms, racisms and other social oppressions must be dealt with through multiple strategies. But we will also have to make specific political choices as to which strategy we are going to identify with in the struggle against social oppressions. For example, choosing to focus on anti-Black racism does not by itself negate the struggle against anti-Semitism. They are both forms of racism that an anti-racism struggle has to confront. The task is to be able to connect these struggles and also to relate anti-racism with other forms of social oppression and the broader political economic questions.

There are multiple sites of privilege and oppression. Individuals and groups are socially positioned in different ways in terms of privilege and oppression. Therefore, it is possible to be materially privileged and yet oppressed dialectically. For example, it is possible for an upper middle-class Black woman to still face race and gender oppression in society, in spite of her material privilege(s). We can speak about these multiple sites of oppression without necessarily arguing that all oppressions are equal in their material consequences. As argued in Chapter Four, we must recognize the saliency of skin-colour racism as a form of social oppression. As anti-racism workers engage social oppression from multiple racial, class, sexual and gender positions of subordination, domination, privilege and power, we must believe in the power of human agency and community-level organizing to achieve meaningful change.

The issues of social justice, equity and power-sharing are more than moral imperatives. These issues speak to the fundamental nature of social reality and human practices. According to Paulo Freire and his concept of "conscientization," there is an indispensable qualitative dialectic between subjectivity and objectivity in the act of knowing (Freire 1990). We must know and understand reality in order to better transform it. Judith Butler points out that "no subject is its own point of departure" (1992: 9), and that individual subjects experience and understand life within a discursive and material context. Social reality is not independent of human experiences. Economic, cultural, political and ideological forces, structures and contexts explain the concrete experiences of daily life. These forces also influence and shape the way individuals interpret reality (see Parpart 1995: 16). It is thus important to explore people's views and interpretations of reality, as it is from these that anti-racism theory can be generated for political action.

As a society, we can address questions of social justice, equity and power-sharing by first understanding ourselves and how we see our social obligations and responsibilities. Unfortunately, the new wind of ultra-Right conservatism sweeping across North America has brought with it a redefinition of social obligations and responsibilities. The state is redefining its obligations to the larger citizenry. Individuals are rethinking their responsibilities to each other. In fact, instead of strengthening communities, we are weakening them. We are not working across our differences. We are pitting groups and communities against each other. We are scapegoating the poor, the weak and the least privileged in our society.

Losing sight of the larger socio-political structures and contexts in which human lives are shaped can only serve to exacerbate the problem of social injustice. We must approach the solution to human problems through a critical examination of how micro- and macro-structures of power and privilege work in society. In the schools, workplaces and organizational settings, to share power and privilege ensures the opening up of spaces for alternative viewpoints to flourish. Sharing power does not entail total or irretrievable loss for the dominant in society. As Fumia (1995) asserts, it should be possible to lose something and gain at the same time.

This book has focused on anti-racism as a political and educational act. Race figures very prominently in Euro-Canadian/American social relations. The tendency to deny or resist race as a powerful organizing principle and tool of social relations is acutely problematic. The notion of race is not only an important factor for the distribution of material and economic goods, it is also a basis for political mobilization. Race relations are not simply personal relations. They are relations of power, identity, conflict and change. Conventional public discourses constantly point to differences within groups who supposedly share culture and race attributes. It is repeatedly argued that the "community" is becoming more and more heterogenous to the extent that there are actually no communities. In such a context it is problematic to speak of identity interests and identity loyalties. And the state in the North American context has been quick to exploit this tension to serve its own material and ideological interests and to weaken the collective struggle for social change.

The politics of anti-racism change must be able to respond to such challenges. Anti-racism must draw on the connections between the individual and community to articulate the possibility and limitations of social transformation. The argument for engaging in a politics of identity can be made along several lines. I devote the remaining pages of this book to this issue. At one level, it is through the individual that the notion of race identity is rendered meaningful. Conversely, through an understanding of the community, individual identities can transcend the boundaries of race, gender, class and sexuality. An examination of how colonial and capitalist hegemony and imperial domination work in concert, for example, helps us to recognize how race and racial identities shape individual and group lives in specific historical contexts. The process of European colonization on non-European peoples and the relationship to racialized discourses is significant for developing a strong critique of minority schooling and education in North American contexts.

Furthermore, the shift from an individual to a collective politics for social change is rendered meaningful if individuals who are engaged in the act of change see themselves as sharing some affinity. This is important given that in the anti-racism movement there have been calls to abandon identity politics in favour of a situational, broad-based politics. Cindy Patton has asked whether "identities" rather than "social practices" can be the foundation for activism (quoted in Britzman 1993: 124). I would say: "both." It is important that we speak of the broader issues that transcend identities and allegiances, that is, that we oppose the larger tyrannies of the state and globalization, such as unemployment, homelessness, poverty and human deprivation.[4] We can only succeed in doing so if we are rooted in a firm identification of self and the group. In other words, the notion of race, class and gender identities is the bedrock on which to build broad-based coalitions for social activism.

However, we should not expect everyone to identify with a particular race, class or gender group. Neither should it be assumed that race politics will naturally be the preferred politics. Similarly, just because the Black community is not a homogenous group (and certainly not all Africans identify with it) does not mean that some Black or African peoples cannot engage in a politics of change starting from a Black/African oppositional or counter culture. To do so is not to particularize racism. It means finding an entry point, in the politics of identity, from which to negotiate power differences among and between groups, and to develop broad-based coalitions as communities of difference and resistance.

Social identity also operates in the politics of transformation. Knowledge and social practices are understood in relation to one's subject position and interests. The notion of identity cannot, therefore, be dismissed in a progressive politics of social change. An appreciation of the relationship between knowledge and identity helps us understand how oppression manifests itself in the attempt to preserve knowledge about ourselves and the identities so constructed and constituted. For example, as Morrison (1992) argues, positive self-identity is secured through reciprocal position within discourses of negation, invisibility, and "foil" identities for the "other." Positive aspects of the self are defined by contrast (or binary oppositional logic) to negative aspects and evaluation of the other (see Taylor 1995).[5] It is this seriously flawed linkage that makes it possible for White society to connect race and crime. A progressive politics of anti-racism change cannot dismiss such social constructions of group identity by simplistically arguing out identity formation in social movement praxis.

Conclusion

Let me conclude by reiterating some important points made earlier. Anti-racism, as a practice of educational change, is concerned with what education ought to, and can look like. The focus is on the vision of education that acknowledges that one cannot articulate and fight for social change without an understanding of the current social and political order. How we name issues reflects our degree of comprehension of the problem. At this historical juncture we also need to ask whether everything that has been called "anti-racism" is really anti-racism. I call on all progressive educators who hesitate to call themselves "anti-racist" to examine their educational practice to see whether they are in fact "non-racist" or "anti-racist" educators. There is a qualitative difference and distinction in that anti-racism is proactive. It is action-oriented education committed to social change. The "non-racist" position does not implicate one in working pro-actively for change.

Educators and administrators will have to redouble their efforts to make educational excellence accessible to all students. Anti-racism educators need to work hard to promote and guarantee equitable education outcomes for all. It is not going to be easy. But it is important that we as a society recognize that there is a social and economic cost to every form of educational and social inequity. As schools respond to challenges of difference and diversity the slogan must be that being "different" is not the "problem." Different does not, and should not, mean "unequal" or "incapable." Schools can nurture a "community of differences" by helping all students and teachers to affirm, relate, define, interpret, explain and negotiate social differences in positive ways. Teachers can begin to unlearn social stereotypes and champion the cause of the "voices of difference." They can begin to challenge the knowledge encoded as authentic and sacred in the text and the "deep" curriculum. Administrators can also provide the tools and resources to assist schools and teachers in this challenge. As members of society, we can all play our respective roles to ensure that we live the ideal of an economically, socially, culturally and politically democratic society. But, I would stress that it is the teacher's responsibility to provide the best education possible for her or his students. Anti-racism education allows this to happen. Anti-racism education is good education in that it meets individual and group needs.

We live in a time of great uncertainty. The pressures and challenges of sharing wealth and power are more profound now than ever before. Economic, political and cultural changes in the world have brought forth unprecedented changes in the way we live together and share space and material resources. The effects of a globalized hegemony of Western industrial capital on modern societies are astounding. I refer in particular to the global presence of capital in all available geographical spaces, or what Ahmad (1995) aptly sees as a globalized market place resulting from the penetration of imperialist capital into every global space. Current global economic restructuring processes have intensified human misery and economic deprivation among and between social groups, communities and nation states. The transnationalization of capital has also been accompanied by mass population movements, as well as information flow across nations and territories. Euro-Canadian/American political and economic hegemony is continually reproduced through the use of Western capital and resources (education, mass media, wealth) to establish a Eurocentric view of the world as inclusive and universal (see Giroux 1981). All this presents a challenge; we need to adopt an internationalistic approach to anti-racism education and politics. In other words, new critical approaches to anti-racism studies must theorize social change beyond the boundaries of race, nations and communities.

Notes

1. Historically, passing referred to the process where Black slaves would use their ability to pass as Whites to gain freedom, and then later to live in the mainstream White "world" to avoid persecution. More generally, passing now refers to the process where women can gain access and become successful in the corporate world, or to people of colour who can "pass" as White.

2. The populist politics of race baiting is directed and sustained by a powerful segment of public opinion. There is fear of an emerging assault on the established order and a sense that it must be defended. It is becoming easier to jump on what I would call the "race critique bandwagon," because the current climate of ultra-conservatism and fiscal constraint dictates that as a society we must be prudent and tough; thus, we must defend the prevailing social order before it is lost. Society cannot allow "free loaders" on the system. Attempts to "rock the boat" ought to be checked. This is demanded by the public. Everyone must find or pay his or her own way. And that means individual achievement and merit principles must apply to the tee. Rather than examining systemic unfairness and instituting equity measures to address historic or collective wrongs, the state through its institutions must redefine responsibilities and obligations, and protect the established order of things.

3. For example, some Canadians saw the Rodney King beating in Los Angeles and the subsequent riots as something that can only happen in the United States. It was an epitome of how bad race relations had become in the US relative to Canada. So, when youths went on a rampage on Yonge Street in Toronto on 4 May 1992, the reference point for public discussion in some Canadian circles was how worse things are in the US. Similarly, following the O.J. Simpson verdict in 1995, it was not uncommon for some Canadians to point out that Simpson's acquittal could not have happened in Canada because the verdict was more a reflection on the extent of racism in the US.

4. See CARF. 1995. "Commentary," "UK: Fighting Our Fundamentalisms: An Interview With A. Sivanandan by CARF 73." *Race & Class* 36(3): 73-81.

5. For instance, historically, the ethnocentricism and racism of early European travellers and missionaries (in their first contact with African and other colonized peoples) led to a construction of the "superiority" of Europeans and their cultures. This was accomplished through a negation and devaluation of African and other colonized peoples. Today, the criminalization of Black youth is similarly accomplished within a subordinated racialized identity. For Black peoples, a location/contextualization in historic and contemporary constructions of racialized and subordinated identities provides the impetus to engage in a critical political praxis to challenge a continuing racial oppression.

References

Abdo, Nahla. 1993. "Race, Gender and Politics: The Struggle of Arab Women in Canada." In Linda Carty (ed.), *And Still We Rise: Feminist Political Mobilizing in Contemporary Canada*. Toronto: Women's Press, pp. 73–98.

Abella, R. 1984. *Equality: Report of the Special Committee on Visible Minorities in Canadian Society*. Ottawa: Queen's Printer.

Adorno, T., Else Frenkel-Brunswik, Daniel Levinson and R. Nevitt-Sanford. 1950. *The Authoritarian Personality Part 1 & 11*. New York: John Wiley and Sons.

Ahmad, Aijaz. 1995. "The Politics of Literary Post-Coloniality." *Race & Class* 36(3): 1–20.

Alladin, I. (ed.). 1995. *Racism in Canadian Schools*. Toronto: Harcourt Brace Canada.

Allport, G. 1954. *The Nature of Prejudice*. Cambridge, MA: Addison-Wesley.

Amin, Samir. 1994. "Ideology and Social Thought: The Intelligentsia and the Development Crisis." *Codesria Bulletin* 3: 15–23.

Amos, Y. and P. Parmar. 1987. "Resistance and Responses: The Experiences of Black Girls in Britain." In M. Arnot and G. Weiner (eds.), *Gender and the Politics of Schooling*. London: Hutchinson, pp. 211–22.

Anthias, F. and Nira Yuval-Davis. 1983. "Contextualizing Feminisms: Gender Ethnic and Class Division." *Feminist Review* 15: 62–75.

———. 1992. *Racialized Boundaries: Race, Nation, Gender, Colour and Class and the Anti-Racist Struggle*. New York: Routledge.

Apple, Michael. 1986. *Teachers and Texts: A Political Economy of Class and Gender Relations in Education*. New York: Routledge and Kegan Paul.

———. 1989. "American Realities: Poverty, Economy and Education." In Lois Weis, Eleanor Farrar and Hugh Petrie (eds.), *Dropouts from School*. New York: State University of New York Press, pp. 205–23.

———. 1993. "Rebuilding Hegemony: Education, Equality, and the New Right." In Dennis Dworkin and Leslie Roman (eds.), *Views Beyond the Border Country*. New York: Routledge, pp. 91–114.

——— and J. Taxel. 1982. "Ideology and the Curriculum." In A. Hartnett (ed.), *Educational Studies and Social Science*. London: Heinemann, pp. 166–78.

Asante, Molefi K. 1991. "The Afrocentric Idea in Education." *Journal of Negro Education* 60(2): 170–80.

Ayittey, George. 1991. *Indigenous African Institutions*. Ardsley-on-Hudson, NY: Transnational Publishers.

Bains, H. and P. Cohen. 1988. *Multiracist Britain*. London: MacMillan.

Banks, Curtis. W. 1992. "The Theoretical and Methodological Crisis of the Africentric Conception." *Journal of Negro Education* 61(3): 262–72.

Anti-Racism Education

Banks, James. 1992. "Multicultural Education: For Freedom's Sake." *Educational Leadership* 49(4): 32–36.

——. 1993. "The Canon Debate, Knowledge Construction and Multicultural Education." *Educational Researcher* 22(5): 4–14.

——. 1994a. "The Historical Reconstruction of Knowledge About Race: The Implication for Transformative Teaching." Paper read at the Annual Meeting of the American Educational Research Association, New Orleans, LA, April 4–9.

——. 1994b. "Transforming the Mainstream Curriculum." *Educational Leadership* 51(8): 4–8.

——. 1995. Presentation at the symposium on "Teaching Culturally Different Students: Political Assumptions of the Educational Research." Annual Meeting of the American Educational Research Association, San Francisco, April 18–22.

Bannerji, Himani. 1991a. "But Who Speaks for Us?: Experience and Agency in Conventional Feminist Paradigms." In Himani Bannerji, Linda Carty, Kari Dehli, Susan Heald and Kate McKenna (eds.), *Unsettling Relations: The University as a Site of Feminist Struggles*. Toronto: Women's Press, pp. 67–108.

——. 1991b. "Racism, Sexism, Knowledge and the Academy." *Resources for Feminist Research* 20(3/4): 5–12.

——. (ed.), 1993. *Returning the Gaze: Essays on Racism, Feminism and Politics*. Toronto: Sister Vision Press.

Banton, Michael. 1967. *Racial Consciousness*. London: Longman's.

——. 1977. *The Idea of Race*. London: Tavistock.

——. 1979. "Analytical and Folk Concepts of Race and Ethnicity." *Ethnic and Racial Studies* 2: 127–38.

Barth, F. 1969. *Ethnic Groups and Boundaries*. Boston: Little Brown.

Battiste, Marie and Jean Barman (eds.). 1995. *First Nations Education in Canada: The Circle Unfolds*. Vancouver: University of British Columbia Press.

Behdad, Ali. 1993. "Travelling to Teach: Post Colonial Critics in the American Academy." In Cameron McCarthy and Warren Crichlow (eds.), *Race, Identity and Representation in Education*. New York: Routledge, pp. 40–9.

Belkhir, Jean and Michael Ball. 1993. "Editor's Introduction: Integrating Race, Sex and Class in our Disciplines." *Race, Sex and Class* 1(1): 3–11.

——, Susan Griffith, Christine Sleeter and C. Allsup. 1994. "Race, Sex, Class and Multicultural Education: Women's Angle of Vision." *Race, Sex and Class* 1(2): 7–22.

Benn, Ellie 1995. "Reflections of a First Year Student Teacher." Unpublished paper, Department of Sociology in Education, Ontario Institute for Studies in Education, Toronto.

Bhabha, Homi. 1990. *Nation and Narration*. London: Routledge.

——. 1991. "The Other Question: Difference, Discrimination and the Discourse of Colonialism." In R. Ferguson, M. Gever, Trinh T. Minha and Cornel West (eds.), *Out There: Marginalization and Contemporary Cultures*. Cambridge, MA: MIT Press, pp. 71–88.

——. 1994. *The Location of Culture*. London: Routledge.

Bhyat, Alice. 1993. "Bias in the Curriculum: A Comparative Look at Two Boards of Education." Unpublished major research paper, Department of Sociology in Education, Ontario Institute for Studies in Education, Toronto.

Biddiss, M. 1979. "Towards a History of European Racism." *Ethnic and Racial Studies*

References

2(4): 508–13.

Black Educators Working Group (BEWG). 1993. *Submission to the Ontario Royal Commission on Learning.* Toronto: Black Educators Working Group.

Board of Education, Toronto. 1988. *Education of Black Students in Toronto: Final Report of the Consultative Committee.* Toronto: Board of Education.

Bolaria, S. and P. Li (eds.). 1988. *Racial Oppression in Canada.* Toronto: Garamond.

Borg, Carmel. 1995. "Hegemony as Educational Practice." Ph.D. dissertation, Department of Education, University of Toronto, Toronto.

Bourdieu, Pierre. 1970. *La Reproduction: Elements pour une Systeme d'Enseignement.* Paris: Edition de Minuit.

Bourne, Jenny. 1987. *Homelands of the Mind: Jewish Feminism and Identity Politics.* London: The Institute of Race Relations, Race and Class Pamphlet No. 11.

Bowles, S. and H. Gintis. 1976. *Schooling in Capitalist America.* New York: Basic Books.

Brah, A. 1993. "Re-Framing Europe: En-gendered Racisms, Ethnicities and Nationalisms in Contemporary Western Europe." *Feminist Review* 45: 9–28.

Brand, Dionne and Krisantha Sri Bhaggiyadatta. 1986. *Rivers have Sources, Trees have Roots, Speaking of Racism.* Toronto: Cross Cultural Communication Centre.

Brandt, Geoffrey. 1986. *The Realization of Anti-Racist Teaching.* London: Falmer Press.

Brathwaite, Keren. 1989. "The Black Student and the School: A Canadian Dilemma." In S. Chilingu and S. Niang (eds.), *African Continuities/L'Héritage Africain.* Toronto: Terebi, pp. 195–216.

Bray, M., P.B. Clarke and D. Stephens. 1986. *Education and Society in Africa.* London: Edward Arnold, pp. 101–13.

Brewer, Rose M. 1993. "Theorizing Race, Class and Gender: The New Scholarship of Black Feminist Intellectuals and Black Women's Labour." In Stanlie James and Abena Busia (eds.), *Theorizing Black Feminisms.* New York: Routledge, pp. 13–30.

Britzman, Deborah. 1993. "The Ordeal of Knowledge: Rethinking the Possibilities of Multicultural Education." *Review of Education* 15: 123–35.

———. 1995. "Is There a Queer Pedagogy? Or, Stop Reading Straight." *Educational Theory* 45(2): 151–65.

Brown, Robert. 1993. *A Follow-Up of the Grade 9 Cohort of 1987 Every Secondary Student Survey Participants.* Toronto Board of Education, Research Report #207.

Brown, Robert, Maisy Cheng, Maria Yau and Suzanne Ziegler. 1992. *The 1991 Every Secondary Student Survey: Initial Findings.* Toronto: Toronto Board of Education.

Bulham, H.A. 1985. *Frantz Fanon and the Psychology of Oppression.* New York: Plenum Press.

Bunch, C. 1987. *Passionate Politics: Feminist Theory and Action.* New York: St. Martin's Press.

Burbules, N.C. and S. Rice. 1991. "Dialogue Across Difference: Continuing the Conversation." *Harvard Educational Review* 61(4): 393–416.

Butler, Judith. 1992. "Contingent Foundations: Feminism and the Question of 'Postmodernism.'" In Judith Butler and Joan Scott (eds.), *Feminists Theorize the Political.* London: Routledge, pp. 3–21.

——— and Joan Wallach Scott (eds.). 1992. *Feminists Theorize the Political.* London: Routledge.

Byrne, S. 1994. "Rethinking the Curriculum: The Challenges of Inclusion." Unpublished term paper, Department of Sociology in Education, Ontario Institute for Studies in Education, Toronto.

Calliste, Agnes. 1991. "Canada's Immigration Policy and Domestics from the Caribbean." *Socialist Studies* 5: 136–68.

———. 1993a. "Race, Gender and Canadian Immigration Policy." *Journal of Canadian Studies* 28(4): 131–48.

———. 1993b. "Women of Exceptional Merit: Immigration of Caribbean Nurses to Canada." *Canadian Journal of Women and the Law* 6(1): 85–102.

———. 1994a. "Race, Gender and Canadian Immigration Policy: Blacks from the Caribbean 1900-1932." *Journal of Canadian Studies* 28(4): 131–47.

———. 1994b. "Anti-Racist Educational Initiatives in Nova Scotia." *Orbit* 25(2): 48–49.

———. 1994c. "Blacks' Struggle for Education Equity in Nova Scotia." In Vincent D'Oyley (ed.), *Black Innovations in Canadian Education.* Toronto: Umbrella Press.

Campbell, P.B. and J. Wirtenberg. 1980. "How Books Influence Children: What the Research Shows." *Interracial Books for Children Bulletin* 11(6): 3–6.

Canadian Alliance of Black Educators (CABE). 1992. *Sharing The Challenge I, II, III: A Focus on Black High School Students.* Toronto: Canadian Alliance of Black Educators.

Caraway, Nancie. 1991. *Segregated Sisterhood: Racism and the Politics of American Feminism.* Knoxville: University of Tennessee Press.

Carby, Hazel. 1982a. "White Women Listen! Black Feminism and the Boundaries of Sisterhood." In Paul Gilroy/Centre for Contemporary Cultural Studies (ed.), *The Empire Strikes Back.* London: Hutchinson, pp. 212–35.

———. 1982b. "Schooling for Babylon." In Paul Gilroy/Centre for Contemporary Cultural Studies (ed.). *The Empire Strikes Back.* London: Hutchison, pp. 183–211.

———. 1992. "The Multicultural Wars. " In G. Dent (ed.), *Black Popular Culture.* New York: Dia Center for the Arts, pp. 181–99.

Carty, Linda. 1991a. "Black Women in Academia." In Himani Bannerji, Linda Carty, Kari Dehli, Susan Heald and Kate McKenna (eds.), *Unsettling Relations.* Toronto: Women's Press, pp. 13–44.

———. 1991b. "Women's Studies in Canada: A Discourse and Praxis of Exclusion." *Resources for Feminist Research* 20(3/4): 12–18.

———. 1993. "Introduction: Combining our Efforts: Making Feminism Relevant to the Changing Sociality." In Linda Carty (ed.), *And Still We Rise: Feminist Political Mobilizing in Contemporary Canada.* Toronto: Women's Press, pp. 7–21.

Castagna, M. 1994. "Blacks in Education: A Ticket to Somewhere." *The Akili Newsletter* 1(4): 3–6.

Castenell, L.A. and W.F. Pinar (eds.). 1993. *Understanding Curriculum as Racial Text: Representations of Identity and Difference in Education.* Albany: SUNY Press.

Cheng, Maisy. 1995. "Black Youth and Schooling in the Canadian Context: A Focus on Ontario." Unpublished paper, Department of Sociology in Education, Ontario Institute for Studies in Education, Toronto.

———, Gerry Tsuji, Maria Yau and Suzanne Ziegler. 1993. *The Every Secondary Student Survey, Fall, Part II: Detailed Profiles of Toronto's Secondary School Students.* Toronto: Toronto Board of Education.

Chilungu, Simeon W. and Sada N'iang. 1989. *African Continuities/L'Héritage Africain.* Toronto: Terebi.

Codjoe, Henry M. 1995. "Experiences of Black/African-Canadian High School Graduates in Alberta's Public School System: A Multi-Case Study." Ph.D. research proposal, Department of Education Policy Studies, University of Alberta.

References

Cohen, Philip. 1988/9. *Tackling Common Sense Racism. Cultural Studies Project Annual Report.* London: Cultural Studies Project.
———. 1989. "Reason, Racism and the Popular Monster." In B. Richards (ed.). *Crises of the Self.* London: Free Association Books.
Collins, Emma. 1994. "Black Focused Schools: An Examination." *Pride Magazine* 3: 23–24.
Collins, Patricia Hill. 1990. *Black Feminist Thought.* London: Harper Collins.
———. 1993. "Toward a New Vision: Race, Class and Gender as Categories of Analysis and Connection." *Race, Sex and Class* 1(1): 25–45.
Combahee River Collective. 1981. "Combahee River Collective Statement." In C. Moraga and G. Anzaldua (eds.), *This Bridge Called My Back.* New York: Kitchen Table-Women of Color Press. pp. 210–220.
Comer, J.P. 1988. "Educating Poor Minority Children." *Scientific American* 259(5): 42–48.
Cornbleth, C. and D. Waugh. 1993. "The Great Speckled Bird: Education Policy-in-the-Making." *Educational Researcher* 22(7): 31–37.
Cox, Oliver. 1948. *Caste, Class and Race: A Study in Social Dynamics.* New York: Monthly Review Press.
———. 1976. *Race Relations: Elements and Social Dynamics.* Detroit: Wayne State University Press.
Curtis Bruce, David Livingstone and Harry Smaller. 1992. *Stacking The Deck: The Streaming of Working Class Kids in Ontario Schools.* Toronto: Our Schools Our Selves.
Daenzer, Patricia and George J.S. Dei. 1994. "Issues of School Completion/Dropout: A Focus on Black Youth in Ontario Schools and Relevant Studies." Background paper submitted to the Ontario Royal Commission on Learning, Toronto.
Dahan, Carole. 1992. "Spheres of Identity: Feminism and Difference: Notes by a Sephardic Jewess." *Fireweed* 35: 46–50.
Daigre, B. 1994. "Implementing the Afrocentric School: Challenges and Successes." An address to the National Council of Black Educators of Canada. Annual Meeting, Chateau Halifax Hotel, Halifax, Nova Scotia, May 13.
Deckha, Nityanand. 1994. Personal communication. Department of Sociology in Education, Ontario Institute for Studies in Education, Toronto.
Dehli, Kari. 1994. "Parent Activism and School Reform in Toronto." Report submitted to the Ontario Ministry of Education and Training, Toronto.
———, J. Restakis and Errol Sharpe. 1988. "The Rise and Fall of the Toronto Parents' Movement." In F. Cunningham, S. Findlay, M. Kadar, A. Lennon and E. Silva (eds.), *Socialist Studies Annual.* Toronto: Between the Lines; pp. 209–27.
Dei, George J.S. 1993. "The Challenges of Anti-Racist Education in Canada." *Canadian Ethnic Studies* 25(2): 36–51.
———. 1994a. "The Women of a Ghanaian Village: A Study of Social Change." *African Studies Review* 37(2): 121–45.
———. 1994b. "Reflections of An Anti-Racist Pedagogue." In Lorna Erwin and David MacLennan (eds.), *The Sociology of Education in Canada.* Toronto: Copp Clark Pitman, pp. 290–310.
———. 1994c. "Afrocentricity: A Cornerstone of Pedagogy." *Anthropology and Education Quarterly* 25(1): 3–28.
———, L. Holmes, J. Mazzuca, E. McIsaac and R. Campbell. 1995. "Push Out or Drop

Out?: The Dynamics of Black/African-Canadian Students' Disengagement from School." Final report submitted to the Ontario Ministry of Education and Training, Toronto.

————. 1995. "Examining the Case for African-Centred Schools in Ontario." *McGill Journal of Education* 30(2): 179–98.

———— and Sherene Razack. 1995. "Inclusive Schooling: An Inventory of Contemporary Practices Designed to Meet the Challenge of a Diverse Student Body." Report submitted to the Ontario Ministry of Education and Training, Toronto.

Derrida, J. 1978. *Writing and Difference*. London: Routledge.

Dijk, Teun A. van. 1993. *Elite Discourse and Racism*. London: Sage.

Dill, B.T. and M.B. Zinn. 1990. *Race and Gender: Re-visioning Social Relations*. Memphis, TN: Center for Research on Women, Memphis State University, Research Paper Number 11.

Dines, G. 1994. "What's Left of Multiculturalism?: Race, Class, Gender in the Classroom." *Race, Sex and Class* 1(2): 23–34.

Dollard, J. 1939. *Caste and Class in a Southern Town*. New York: Doubleday.

Donald, James and Ali Rattansi (eds.). 1992. *Race, Culture and Difference*. Newbury Park, CA: Sage.

Doyle, Marie. 1995. "Gap in the Vision, Gulfs in the Promise: An Anti-Racist Critique of Culture-Based Schooling in the N.W.T." Unpublished paper, Department of Sociology in Education, Ontario Institute for Studies in Education, Toronto.

D'Oyley, Vincent. 1994. *Black Innovations in Canadian Education*. Toronto: Umbrella Press.

Elias, Norman. 1978. *What is Sociology?* London: Hutchinson.

Ellsworth, Elizabeth. 1992. "Why Doesn't This Feel Empowering: Working Through The Repressive Myths of Critical Pedagogy." In C. Luke and J. Gore (eds.), *Feminisms and Critical Pedagogy*. New York: Routledge.

Erickson, Fred. 1987. "Transformation and School Success: The Politics and Culture of Educational Achievement." *Anthropology and Education* 18(4): 335–56.

Ernst, Gisela and F. Statzner. 1994. "Alternative Vision of Schooling: An Introduction." *Anthropology and Education Quarterly* 25(3): 200–07.

————, Elza Statzner and Henry T. Trueba. 1994. "Alternative Visions of Schooling: Success Stories in Minority Settings." *Anthropology and Education Quarterly* 25(3) (Special Issue). pp 200–394.

Essed, Philomena. 1990. *Everyday Racism Reports from Women of Two Cultures*. Alameda, CA: Hunter House.

Estrada, K. and P. McLaren. 1993. "A Dialogue on Multiculturalism and Democratic Culture." *Educational Researcher* 22(3): 27–33.

Eyoh, Dickson. 1995. "From the Belly to the Ballot: Ethnicity and Politics in Africa." *Queen's Quarterly* 102(1): 39–48.

Fanon, Frantz. 1967. *Black Skin, White Masks*. New York: Grove.

Farrell, Vernon. 1994. "Support for Black Focused Schools." *Share* January 6: 8.

Figueroa, Peter. 1991. *Education and the Social Construction of 'Race.'* London: Routledge, Chapman and Hall.

Fine, Michelle. 1991. *Framing Dropouts: Notes on the Politics of Urban Public High School*. New York: State University of New York Press.

Fordham, Signithia. 1988. "Racelessness as a Factor in Black Students' School Success: Pragmatic Strategy or Pyrrhic Victory?" *Harvard Educational Review* 58(1): 54–84.

References

Foucault, Michel. 1980. *Power/Knowledge: Selected Interviews 1972–77.* Edited by C. Gordon. Brighton: Harvester Press.

Frankenberg, Ruth. 1993a. *The Social Construction of Whiteness: White Women, Race Matters.* Minneapolis: University of Minnesota Press.

———. 1993b. "Growing Up White: Feminism, Racism, and the Social Geography of Childhood." *Feminist Review* 45: 51–84.

Franz, C. and A. Stewart. 1994. *Women Creating Lives: Identity, Resilience and Resistance.* Boulder, CO: Westview Press.

Freire, Paulo. 1990. *Pedagogy of the Oppressed.* New York: Continuum.

Fumia, Doreen. 1995. "Identifying Sites of Anti-Racism Education. Everyday Lived Experiences Seen as the Micro-Politics of Institutionalized Racialized Practices." Unpublished paper, Department of Sociology in Education, Ontario Institute for Studies in Education, Toronto.

Fuss, Diana. 1989. *Essentially Speaking: Feminism, Nature and Differemce.* New York: Routledge.

Gabriel, John and Gideon Ben-Tovim. 1979. "The Conceptualization of Race Relations in Sociological Theory." *Ethnic and Racial Studies* 2(2): 190–212.

Garibaldi, A.M. 1992. "Educating and Motivating African-American Males to Succeed." *Journal of Negro Education* 61(1): 4–11.

Gillborn, David. 1995a. "Racism, Modernity and Schooling: New Directions in Anti-racist Theory and Practice." Paper read at the American Educational Research Association, San Francisco, April 18–22.

———. 1995b. *Racism and Anti-racism in Real Schools.* Philadelphia: Open University Press.

Gilroy, Paul (and Centre for Contemporary Cultural Studies) (ed.). 1982. *The Empire Strikes Back: Race and Racism in 70s Britain.* London: Hutchison.

———. 1992. "The End of Anti-Racism." In James Donald and Ali Rattansi (eds.), *'Race' Culture and Difference.* Newbury Park, CA: Sage, pp. 49–61.

———. 1993a. *The Black Atlantic: Modernity and Double Consciousness.* Cambridge: Harvard University Press.

———. 1993b. *Small Acts: Thoughts on the Politics of Black Cultures.* London: Serpent's Tail.

Giroux, Henry. 1981. *Ideology and Culture and the Process of Schooling.* Philadelphia: Temple University Press.

———. 1983a. *A Theory of Resistance in Education: A Pedagogy for the Opposition.* South Hadley, MA: Bergin and Harvey.

———. 1983b. "Theories of Reproduction and Resistance in the New Sociology of Education." *Harvard Educational Review* 53(3): 257–93.

———. 1984. "The Paradox of Power in Educational Theory and Practice." *Language Arts* 61: 462–65.

———. 1986. "Radical Pedagogy and the Politics of Student Voice." *Interchange* 17: 48–69.

———. 1992a. "Post-colonial Ruptures and Democratic Possibilities: Multiculturalism as Anti-Racist Pedagogy." *Cultural Critique* 21: 5–39.

———. 1992b. "Resisting Difference: Cultural Studies and the Discourse of Critical Pedagogy." In Lawrence Grossberg, Cary Nelson and Paul Treichler (eds.), *Cultural Studies.* New York: Routledge, pp. 199–212.

———. 1994. "Insurgent Multiculturalism and the Promise of Pedagogy." In David T.

Goldberg (ed.), *Multiculturalism: A Critical Reader*. London: Blackwell, pp. 325–43.

Goldberg, David T. 1993. *Racist Culture*. Oxford: Blackwell.

——— and Abebe Zegeye. 1995. "Editorial Note." *Social Identities* 1(1): 3–4.

Gordon, Beverly. 1990. "The Necessity of African-American Epistemology for Educational Theory." *Journal of Education* 173(3): 89–106.

Grant, Agnes. 1995. "The Challenge for Universities." In Marie Battiste and Jean Barman (eds.), *First Nations Education in Canada: The Circle Unfolds*. Vancouver: University of British Columbia Press, pp. 208–223.

Greene, M. 1994. "Beginnings, Identities and Possibilities: The Uses of Social Imagination." Paper read at the American Educational Researchers Association (AERA), Annual Meeting, New Orleans, LA, April 4–8.

Grewal, Inderpal and Caren Kaplan. 1994. "Introduction: Transnational Feminist Practices and Questions of Postmodernity." In Inderpal Grewal and Caren Kaplan (eds.), *Scattered Hegemonies*. Minneapolis: University of Minnesota Press.

Gupta, Akhil and James Ferguson. 1992. "Beyond 'Culture': Race, Identity and the Politics of Difference." *Cultural Anthropology* 7(1): 6–23.

Gyekye, Kwame. 1987. *An Essay in African Philosophical Thought*. London: Cambridge University Press.

Hall, Budd. 1993. "Introduction." In P. Pak, M. Brydon-Miller, Budd Hall and Ted Jackson (eds.), *Voices of Change: Participatory Research in the United States and Canada*. Toronto: OISE Press, pp. xiii–xxii.

Hall, Stuart. 1979. "Ethnicity: Identity and Experience." *Radical America* Summer (1979): 9–20.

———. 1988. *Problems in Anti-Racist Strategy*. London: Runnymeade.

———. 1991. "Old and New Identities: Old and New Ethnicities." In A. King (ed.), *Culture, Globalization and the World System*. New York: State University Press, pp. 41–68.

Harris, C.I. 1993. "Whiteness as Property." *Harvard Law Review* 106(8): 1710–91.

Harris, Michael. 1992. "Africentrism and Curriculum: Concepts, Issues and Prospects." *Journal of Negro Education* 61(3): 301–16.

Henry, Annette. 1992. "Taking Back Control: Toward an Afrocentric Womanist Standpoint on the Education of Black Children." Ph.D. dissertation, Department of Curriculum, Ontario Institute for Studies in Education, Toronto.

———. 1993a. "African-Canadian Women Teachers' Activism: Recreating Communities of Caring and Resistance." *Journal of Negro Education* 61(3): 392–404.

———. 1993b. "Missing: Black Self-Representations in Canadian Educational Research." *Canadian Journal of Education* 18(3): 206–24.

Henry, F., C. Tator, W. Mattis and T. Rees. 1995. *The Colour of Democracy: Racism in Canadian Society*. Toronto: Harcourt Brace.

Herrnstein, K.J. and C. Murray. 1994. *Bell Curve: The Reshaping of American Life By Differences of Intelligence*. New York: Free Press.

Hilliard, Asa. 1992. "Why We Must Pluralize the Curriculum." *Educational Leadership* 49(4): 12–15.

Holmes, Leilani. 1994. "Land, Difference and Identity: A Study of Hawaiian Knowledge Production." Ph.D. research proposal, Department of Sociology in Education, Ontario Institute for Studies in Education, Toronto.

———. 1995. "Elders Knowledge and the Ancestry of Experience in Hawai'i." Paper

References

presented at the Learned Societies Meeting of the Canadian Association for the Study of International Development. Université du Québec, Montréal, June 4–6.

———— and Josephine Mazzuca. 1995. Personal communication. Department of Sociology in Education, Ontario Institute for Studies in Education, Toronto.

Holmes, R.M. 1995. *How Young Children Perceive Race.* Thousand Oaks, CA: Sage.

hooks, bell. 1984. *Feminist Theory: From Margin to Centre.* Boston: South End Press.

————. 1988. *Talking Back: Thinking Feminist, Thinking Black.* Toronto: Between the Lines.

————. 1990. *Yearning: Race, Gender, and Cultural Politics.* Boston: South End Press.

————. 1993. *Sisters of the Yam: Black Women and Self-Recovery.* Toronto: Between the Lines.

————. 1994. *Teaching to Transgress: Education as the Practice of Freedom.* New York: Routledge.

Hountondji, Paul. 1983. *African Philosophy: Myth and Reality.* Bloomington: Indiana University Press.

Hunter, Deborah, A. 1983. "The Rhetorical Challenge of Afro-Centricity." *Western Journal of Black Studies* 7(4): 239–43.

Ibrahim, Awad. 1994. "Hey, Who Said the Road to Freedom is Easy!: Preparing Classrooms for Multiracial, Multicultural Population." Paper presented at the Critical Pedagogy and Cultural Studies Work-in-Progress Seminars, Ontario Institute for Studies in Education, Toronto, November.

International Institute for Advocacy for School Children. 1993. *Academic Discrimination: Failure to Recognize Individual Differences.* Oregon: International Institute for Advocacy for School Children.

International Institute for Global Education (IIGE). 1995. "School Ethos: Principles and Manifestations." Draft report of IIGE, Ontario Green Schools Project. Toronto.

Jacob, E. and C. Jordan (eds.). 1993. *Minority Education: Anthropological Perspectives.* Norwood, NJ: Albex Publishing.

James, Carl. 1990. *Making It: Black Youth, Racism and Career Aspirations in a Big City.* Oakville, ON: Mosaic Press.

————. 1994. "I Don't Want To Talk About It." *Orbit* 25(2): 26–29.

————. 1995. "Multicultural and Anti-Racism Education in the Canadian Context." *Race, Gender and Class* 2(3): 31–48.

Jameson, F., T. Eagleton and E. Said. 1990. *Nationalism, Colonialism and Literature.* Minneapolis: University of Minnesota Press.

Jeffcoate, R. 1984. "Ideologies and Multicultural Education." In M. Craft (ed.), *Education and Cultural Pluralism.* Lewes: Falmer Press.

Joyce, Moon V. 1995a. Class Communication, 1947S: "Principles of Anti-Racism Education." Department of Sociology in Education, Ontario Institute for Studies in Education, Toronto, Spring.

————. 1995b. "Approaches to Anti-Racist/Anti-Oppression Education: Implications for Employment Equity Interventions." Unpublished paper, Department of Sociology in Education, Ontario Institute for Studies in Education, Toronto.

Kailin, J. 1994. "Anti-Racist Staff Development for Teachers: Considerations of Race, Class and Gender." *Teaching and Teacher Education* 10(2): 169–84.

Keto, Tsehloane C. 1990. *The Africa-Centered Perspective of History.* Blackwood, NJ: C.A. Associates.

Khan, Shahnaz. 1995. "Muslim Women: Integrating the Construct in Canada." Ph.D.

dissertation, Department of Sociology in Education, Ontario Institute for Studies in Education, Toronto.

Khayatt, Didi. 1994. "The Boundaries of Identity at the Intersections of Race, Class and Gender." *Canadian Woman Studies: Racism and Gender* 14(2): 6–13.

Kilson, M. 1994. "A Black-American Perspective on All-Black Schools." *The Akili Newsletter: Knowledge Through Time.* 1(4): 14–18.

King, D. 1988. "Multiple Jeopardy, Multiple Consciousness: The Context of a Black Feminist Ideology." *Signs* 14(1): 42–72.

King, Joyce E. 1991. "Dysconscious Racism: Ideology, Identity and Miseducation of Teachers." *Journal of Education* 60(2): 133–46.

————. 1992. "Diaspora Literacy and Consciousness in the Struggle Against Miseducation in the Black Community." *Journal of Negro Education* 61(3): 317–40.

————. 1994. "Perceiving Reality in a New Way: Rethinking the Black/White Duality of our Time." Paper presented at the Annual Meeting of the American Educational Research Association, New Orleans, LA, April 4–9.

Kugler, Jeffrey. 1995a. "Linking the Principles of Anti-Racist Education with the Principles of Global Education." Unpublished major research paper, Department of Education, University of Toronto, Toronto.

————. 1995b. "The Year to Move Forward in the Education of Black Students." Unpublished paper, Department of Sociology in Education, Ontario Institute for Studies in Education, Toronto.

Ladson-Billings, G. 1989. "Like Lightning in a Bottle: Attempting to Capture the Pedagogical Excellence of Successful Teachers of Black Students." Paper presented at the Tenth Annual Urban Ethnography Conference, Philadelphia, PA.

————. 1992. "Liberatory Consequences of Literacy: A Case of Culturally Relevant Instruction for African-American Students." *Journal of Negro Education* 61(3): 378–91.

————. 1994. *The Dreamkeepers. Successful Teachers of African-American Children.* San Francisco: Jossey-Bass Education.

————. 1995. "Comments on the Panel Session: 'African-Centred Education: An Alternative School Model For Meeting the Educational Needs of African-American Students.'" Comments made at the Annual Meeting of the American Educational Research Association, San Francisco, April 18–22.

———— and Annette Henry. 1990. "Blurring the Borders: African Liberatory Pedagogy in the United States and Canada." *Journal of Education* 172(2): 72–88.

Lazreg, M. 1990. "Feminism and Difference: The Perils of Writing as a Woman on Women in Algeria." In M. Hirsch and E.F. Keller (eds.), *Conflicts in Feminism.* New York: Routledge, pp. 326–48.

Le Camp, Lorraine. 1995. "Native and Non-Native Definitions of Self and the Other: Acculturation and Identity Issues in a Duality of Ethnicities." MA thesis proposal, Department of Education, University of Toronto, Toronto.

Leah, Ronnie. 1995. "Anti-Racism Studies: An Integrative Perspective." *Race, Gender and Class* 2(3): 105–22.

Leake, A. and C. Faltz. 1993. "Do we Need to Desegregate all of our Black Schools?" *Educational Policy* 7(3): 370–87.

Lee, Carol D. 1994. "African-Centered Pedagogy: Complexities and Possibilities." In Mwalimu J. Shujaa (ed.), *Too Much Schooling Too Little Education: The Paradox of Black Life in White Societies.* Trenton, NJ: African World Press.

References

Lee, Enid. 1985. *Letters to Marcia: A Teacher's Guide to Anti-Racist Education*. Toronto: Cross-Cultural Communication Centre.

———. 1993. Invited Presentation to a Graduate Class: 1947S: "Principles of Anti-Racist Education." Department of Sociology in Education, Ontario Institute for Studies in Education, Toronto.

———. 1994. "Anti-Racist Education: Panacea or Palliative"? *Orbit* 25(2): 22–5.

Lee-Ferdinand, J. 1994. "Reinventing the Self: The New Post-Colonial Intellectual." Unpublished term paper, Department of Higher Education, Ontario Institute for Studies in Education, Toronto.

Lewington, J. 1995. "Schools More Attuned to Race." *Globe and Mail*, July 10: A4.

Lewis, Oscar. 1969. *A Death in the Sanchez Family*. New York: Random House.

———. 1975. *The Culture of Poverty*. Los Angeles: Pacific Tape.

Lewis, R. 1988. *Anti-Racism: A Mania Exposed*. London: Quartet.

Lewis, S. 1992. *Letter to the Premier: Report on Race Relations in Ontario*. Toronto: Publications Ontario.

Li, Peter S. 1990. "Race and Ethnicity." In Peter Li (ed.), *Race and Ethnic Relations in Canada*. Toronto: Oxford University Press.

——— and Singh Bolaria. 1988. *Racial Oppression in Canada*. Toronto: Garamond Press.

Lightfoot, S. 1980. "Families as Educators: The Forgotten People of Brown." In Derrick Bell (ed.), *Shades of Brown: New Perspectives on School Desegregation*. New York: Teachers College Press, pp. 3–19.

Little, D. 1992. "The Meaning of Yonge Street: What do the Kids Say?" *Our Schools/Our Selves* 4(1): 16–23.

Lomotey, Kofi (ed.). 1990. *Going to School: The African-American Experience*. New York: SUNY Press.

Lorde, Audre. 1984. *Sister Outsider*. Freedom, CA: The Crossing Press.

Macchiusi, J. 1993. "The Origins of Racism and the Rise of Biological Determinism." *Paradox of Racism, Prize Winning Essays* 6: 53–63. Department of Anthropology, York University.

Mackay, Ron and Lawrence Myles. 1989. *Native Student Dropouts in Ontario Schools*. Toronto: Ontario Ministry of Education.

———. 1995. "A Major Challenge for the Education System. Aboriginal Retention and Dropout." In Marie Battiste and Jean Barman (eds.), *First Nations Education in Canada: The Circle Unfolds*. Vancouver: University of British Columbia Press, pp. 157–78.

Madhubuti, H. 1994. "Cultural Work: Planting Trees With New Seeds." In Mwalimu J. Shujaa (ed.), *Too Much Schooling Too Little Education: The Paradox of Black Life In White Societies*. Trenton, NJ: African World Press.

Martin, Denis-Constant. 1995. "The Choices of Identity." *Social Identities* 1(1): 5–20.

Martin, T. 1984. "Why Blacks do Better at Black Colleges." *Ebony* November: 125–28.

Marx, Karl. 1853. "The Future Results of British Rule in India." *New York Daily Tribune* August 8.

Matsuda, Marie. 1989. "When the First Quail Calls: Multiple Consciousness As Jurisprudential Method." *Women Rights Law Reporter* 11(1): 7–10.

May, Stephen. 1994. *Making Multicultural Education Work*. Clevedon: Multilingual Matters Ltd.

Mazrui, A. 1980. *The African Condition*. New York: Cambridge University.

Mbiti, J.S. 1982. "African Views of the Universe." In R. Olaniyan (ed.), *African History and Culture*. Lagos: Longman, pp. 193–99.

McAll, Christopher. 1992. *Class, Ethnicity, and Social Inequality*. Montreal: McGill-Queen's University Press.

McCarthy, Cameron. 1988. "Rethinking Liberal and Radical Perspectives on Racial Inequality in Schooling: Making the Case for Nonsynchrony." *Harvard Educational Review* 58(3): 265–79.

———. 1990. *Race and Curriculum: Social Inequality and the Theory and Politics of Difference in Contemporary Research on Schooling*. London: Falmer Press.

——— and Warren Crichlow (eds.). 1993. *Race, Identity and Representation in Education*. New York: Routledge.

McFadden, A.C. 1992. "A Study of Race and Gender Bias in the Punishment of Handicapped School Children." *Urban Review* 24(4): 239–51.

McIntosh, Peggy. 1990. "White Privilege: Unpacking the Invisible Knapsack." *Independent School* Winter: 31–36.

McIsaac, Elizabeth. 1995. "Indigenous Knowledge and Colonial Power: Locating Resistance and Pedagogical Implications." Paper presented at the Annual Meeting of the Canadian Association of African Studies, Trent University, Peterborough, Ontario, May 10–13.

McLaren, Peter. 1989. *Life in Schools: An Introduction to Critical Pedagogy in the Foundations of Education*. New York: Longman.

———. 1993. *Schooling as a Ritual Performance: Towards a New Political Economy of Symbol and Gesture in Education*. New York: Routledge.

McLeod, J. 1991. "Bridging Street and School." *Journal of Negro Education* 60(3): 260–75.

Memmi, Albert. 1965. *The Colonizer and the Colonized*. Boston: Beacon Press.

Mercer, Kobena and I. Julien. 1988. "Race, Sexual Politics and Black Masculinity: A Dossier." In Rowena Chapman and Jonathan Rutherford (eds.), *Male Order: Unwrapping Masculinity*. London: Lawrence Wishart, pp. 97–164.

Miles, Robert. 1980. "Class, Race and Ethnicity: A Critique of Cox's Theory." *Ethnic and Racial Studies* 3(2): 169–81.

———. 1982. *Racism and Migrant Labour*. London: Routledge and Kegan Paul.

———. 1989. *Racism*. London: Tavistock.

———. 1993. *Racism After "Race Relations."* London: Routledge.

Millet, Kate. 1985. *Sexual Politics*. New York: Ballantine Books.

Ministry of Citizenship. 1989. *Visible Minority Youth Project. Child, Youth and Family Project*. Research Centre, Toronto: Ontario Ministry of Citizenship.

Ministry of Education. 1992. *Changing Perspectives: A Resource Guide for Race and Ethnocultural Equity, K–13*. Toronto: Ontario Ministry of Education.

Ministry of Education and Training (MET). 1993a. *The Common Curriculum, Grades 1–9. Working Document. Version for Parents and the General Public*. Toronto: Ontario Ministry of Education and Training.

———. 1993b. *Anti-Racism and Ethnocultural Equity in School Boards. Guidelines for Policy Development and Implementation*. Toronto: Ontario Ministry of Education and Training.

———. 1993c. *Violence-Free Schools*. Toronto: Ontario Ministry of Education and Training.

Moghissi, Haideh. 1995. "Anti-Racist Feminism: Sisterhood Without White Gloves."

References

Paper read at the Learned Societies Meeting of the Canadian Sociology and Anthropology Association, Université du Québec, Montréal, June 4–7.

Mohanty, Chandra Talpade. 1990. "On Race And Voice: Challenges for Liberal Education in the 90s." *Cultural Critique* 14: 179–208.

———. 1991a. "Cartographies of Struggle," and other selections from Chandra Talpade Mohanty, Ann Russo and Lourdes Torres (eds.), *Third World Women and the Politics of Feminism.* Bloomington: Indiana University Press, pp. 1–47.

———. 1991b. "Under Western Eyes: Feminist Scholarship and Colonial Discourses," In Chandra Talpade Mohanty, Ann Russo and Lourdes Torres (eds.), *Third World Women and the Political of Feminism.* Bloomington: Indiana University Press, pp. 51–80.

Morgan, P.R. and J.M. McPartland. 1981. *The Extent of Classroom Segregation Within Desegregated Schools.* Maryland: National Institute of Education.

Morrison, Toni (ed.). 1992. *Race-ing, Justice, En-gendering Power: Essays on Anita Hill, Clarence Thomas and the Construction of Social Reality.* New York: Pantheon.

Moynihan, Daniel P. 1965. *The Negro Family Case for National Action.* Washington, DC: Labour Department Office and Policy Planning and Research.

Mudimbe, V.J. 1988. *The Invention of Africa: Gnosis, Philosophy and the Order of Knowledge.* Bloomington, IN: Indiana University Press.

———, Kwame Anthony Appiah. 1993. "The Impact of African Studies on Philosophy." In Robert H. Bates, V.H. Mudimbe and Jean O'Barr (eds.), *Africa and the Disciplines.* Chicago: University of Chicago Press, pp. 113–222.

Mukherjee, Alok and Barb Thomas. (n.d.). "A Glossary of Terms." Toronto: Toronto Board of Education.

Mullard, Chris. 1980. *Racism in Society and Schools: History and Policy.* London Centre for Multicultural Education.

———. 1985. *Race, Power and Resistance.* London: Centre for Multicultural Education.

Mullings, Leith. 1992. *Race, Class and Gender: Representations and Reality.* Memphis, TN: Center for Research on Women, Memphis State University.

Muteshi, Jacintha. 1991. "Law, Gender and Power: A Reconstructive and Pedagogical Project." Ph.D. dissertation research proposal, Department of Curriculum, Ontario Institute for Studies in Education, Toronto.

Myrdal, George. 1944. *An American Dilemma: The Negro Problem and Modern Democracy.* New York: Harper and Row.

Nestel, S. 1993. "Facing Foreclosure: A Jew in the Classroom." Department of Adult Education, Ontario Institute for Studies in Education, Toronto, Ontario.

Ng, Roxana. 1988. *The Politics of Community Services: Immigrant Women, Class and the State.* Toronto: Garamond Press.

———. 1993a. "Racism, Sexism and Nation Building in Canada." In Cameron McCarthy and Warren Crichlow (eds.), *Race, Identity and Representation in Education.* New York: Routledge, pp. 50–59.

———. 1993b. "Sexism, Racism, Canadian Nationalism." In Himani Bannerji (ed.), *Returning the Gaze: Essays on Racism, Feminism and Politics.* Toronto: Sister Vision Press, pp. 182–96.

——— and J. Ramirez. 1981. *Immigrant Housewives in Canada.* Toronto: Immigrant Women's Centre.

———, P. Staton and J. Scane (eds.). 1995. *Anti-Racism, Feminism and Critical Approaches to Education.* Toronto: OISE Press.

Anti-Racism Education

Nixon, J. 1984. "Multicultural Education as a Curriculum Category." *New Community* 12: 22–30.

North Carolina Advisory Committee to the U.S. Commission on Civil Rights. 1991. *In-School Segregation in North Carolina Public Schools. A Summary Report.* North Carolina: North Carolina Advisory Committee to the U.S. Commission on Civil Rights.

Novac, Sylvia. 1994. "Boundary Disputes: Sexual Harassment and the Gendered Relations of Residential Tenancy." Ph.D. dissertation, Department of Education, University of Toronto.

Oakes, Jeannie. 1985. *Keeping Track: How Schools Structure Inequality.* New Harlem, CT: Yale University Press.

Okpewho, Isidore. 1992. *African Oral Literature.* Bloomington: Indiana University Press.

Oladipo, O. 1992. *The Idea of African Philosophy: A Critical Study of Major Orientations in Contemporary African Philosophy.* Ibadan: Molecular Publishers.

Oliver, W. 1986. "Black Males and Social Problems: Prevention through Afrocentric Socialization." *Journal of Black Studies* 20(1): 15–39.

———. 1993. "On the Theoretical Concept of Race." In Cameron McCarthy and Warren Crichlow (eds.), *Race, Identity and Representation in Education.* New York: Routledge, pp. 3–10.

Ontario Ministry of Education (OME). 1992. *Changing Perspectives: A Resource Guide for Race and Ethnocultural Equity Education—All Divisions and OACS.* Toronto: Ontario Ministry of Education.

Omi, Michael and Howard Winant. 1993. 2nd edition. *Racial Formation in the United States.* New York: Routledge.

Ong, A. 1988. "Colonialism and Modernity: Feminist Re-presentations of Women in Non-Western Societies." *Inscriptions* 3/4: 79–93.

Parpart, Jane L. 1995. "Is Africa a Postmodern Invention?" *Issue* 23(1): 16–18.

Perrott-Lightning, Elizabeth. 1995. "The Need for Anti-Racist Pedagogy in Approaches to Native Education." Paper delivered at the Learned Societies Meeting of the Canadian Sociology and Anthropology Association, Université du Québec, Montréal, June 4–7.

Philip, M. Nourbese. 1988. *Harriet's Daughter.* Toronto: Women's Press.

———. 1992. *Frontiers: Essays and Writing on Racism and Culture.* Stratford, ON: The Mercury Press.

Pierson, Ruth. 1991. "Experience, Difference, Dominance and Voice in the Writing of Canadian Women's History." In Karen Offen, Ruth Pierson and Jane Randall (eds.), *Writing Women's History: International Perspectives.* Bloomington: Indiana University Press, pp. 79–106.

Powdermaker, H. 1939. *After Freedom: A Cultural Study of the Deep South.* New York: Russell and Russell.

Preudhomme, G.R. 1986. *Black Families: Confronting the Challenge of Education.* New York: New York State Division for Youth.

Purdy, Jared. 1994. "Anti-Racism, Education and Institutional Change: Theoretical Practical Challenges to a Contemporary Crisis." Major paper submitted in partial fulfilment of the award of MA degree in Environmental Studies, York University, Toronto.

Radwanski, George. 1987. *Ontario Study of the Relevance of Education, and the Issue of*

References

Dropouts. Toronto: Ontario Ministry of Education.

Rahim, A. 1990. "Multiculturalism or Ethnic Hegemony: A Critique of Multicultural Education In Toronto." *Journal of Ethnic Studies* 18(3): 29–46.

Rattansi, Ali and Sally Westwood (eds.). 1994. *Racism, Modernity, and Identity*. London: Polity Press.

Ratteray, J. 1990. "African-American Achievement: A Research Agenda Emphasizing Independent Schools." In Kofi Lomotey (ed.), *Going to School: The African-American Experience*. New York: State University of New York Press.

Razack, Sherene. 1994. "What Is to be Gained by Looking White People in the Eye? Culture, Race and Gender of Sexual Violence." *Signs* 19(41): 894–923.

———. 1995a. "Domestic Violence as Gender Persecution: Policing the Borders of Nation, Race and Gender." *Canadian Journal of Women and the Law* 8: 45–88.

———. 1995b. "The Perils of Talking about Culture: Schooling Research in South and East Asian Students." *Race, Gender and Class* 2(3): 67–82.

Reed, Carole-Ann. 1993. "Building Bridges: The Anti-Racist Dimensions of Holocaust Education." Ph.D. dissertation, Department of Education, University of Toronto, Toronto.

———. 1994. "The Omission of Anti-Semitism in Anti-Racism." *Canadian Women Studies*. 14(2): 68–71.

Rethinking Schools. 1991. "An Interview with Educator Enid Lee: Taking Multicultural, Anti-Racist Education Seriously." *Rethinking Schools* 6(1) October–November: 1–4.

Reynolds, L.T. and L. Lieberman. 1993. "The Rise and Fall of 'Race.'" *Race, Sex and Class* 1(1): 109-28.

Rizvi, Fazal. 1995. "Commentary on Panel Session: 'Equity Issues in Education.'" Annual Meeting of the American Educational Research Association, San Francisco, April 18–22.

Rockhill, Kathleen. 1995. "Memo to Adult Education Research Committee." Ontario Institute for Studies in Education, Toronto, Ontario.

Roman, Leslie. 1993. "White is Colour! White Defensiveness, Postmodernism and Anti-racist Pedagogy." In Cameron McCarthy and Warren Crichlow (eds.), *Race, Identity and Representation in Education*. New York: Routledge, pp. 71–88.

Roscigno, Vincent. 1994. "Social Movement Struggle and Race, Gender, Class Inequality." *Race, Sex and Class* 2(1): 109–26.

Royal Commission on Learning (RCOL). 1994. "Equity Considerations." *For the Love of Learning*. Toronto: Queen's Printer of Ontario, pp. 86–98.

Russo, Ann. 1991. "We Cannot Live without Our Lives." In Chandra Mohanty, Ann Russo and Lourdes Torres (eds.), *Third World Women and the Politics of Feminism*. Bloomington: Indiana University Press, pp. 297–313.

Said, Edward. 1979. *Orientalism*. New York: Vintage Books.

———. 1993. *Culture and Imperialism*. New York: Alfred A. Knopf.

Samuels, Jacinth. 1991. "The Sound of Silence: Racism in Contemporary Feminist Theory." MA thesis, Department of Sociology and Anthropology, University of Windsor, Windsor.

Satzewich, Vic. 1990. "The Political Economy of Race and Ethnicity." In Peter Li (ed.), *Race and Ethnic Relations in Canada*. Toronto: Oxford University Press, pp. 209–30.

Scott, Joan W. 1991. "The Evidence of Experience." *Critical Inquiry* 17(3): 773–97.

Anti-Racism Education

————. 1992. "Experience." In J. Butler and J. Scott (eds.), *Feminists Theorize the Political*. London: Routledge, pp. 22–40.

Segrest, M. 1994. *Memoir of a Race Traitor*. Boston: South End Press.

Semali, Ladi and Amy Stambach. 1995. "Cultural Identity in African Context: Indigenous Education and Practice in East Africa." Paper read at the Annual Meeting of the Comparative and International Society, Boston, MA, March 29–April 1.

Shujaa, M. 1994. "Education and Schooling: You Can Have One Without the Other." In Mwalimu J. Shujaa (ed.), *Too Much Schooling Too Little Education: The Paradox of Black Life in White Societies*. Trenton, NJ: African World Press.

Simmel, Georg. 1950. "The Stranger." In K.H. Wolf (ed.), *The Sociology of George Simmel*. New York: The Free Press, pp. 92–96.

Simmons, E. 1994. "Sensitivity Trainers and the Race Thing." *New Internationalist* 260: 26–27.

Sleeter, Christine. 1994. "Multicultural Education, Social Positionality and Whiteness." Paper presented at the Annual Meeting of the American Educational Research Association, New Orleans, LA, April 12–18.

————. 1995. "Teaching Culturally Different Students: Political Assumptions of the Educational Research." Panel session at the Annual Meeting of the American Educational Research Association, San Francisco, April 18–22.

———— and Carl Grant. 1987. "An Analysis of Multicultural Education in the United States." *Harvard Educational Review* 57(4): 421–44.

Solomon, Patrick. 1992. *Black Resistance in High School: Forging a Separatist Culture*. New York: SUNY Press.

Smaller, Harry, Kari Dehli, George Dei, Carl James and Ilda Januario. 1994. "Response to Toronto Board's Study." Submitted to the Race Relations Committee of the Toronto Board of Education, Toronto.

Smith, K.L. 1989. *Teacher Expectations and Minority Achievement: A Study of Black Students in Fairfax County*. Virginia: Fairfax County Schools.

Spivak, Gayatri. 1990. *Post Colonial Critic: Interviews, Strategies, Dialogue*. New York: Routledge.

————. 1993. *Outside in the Teaching Machine*. New York: Routledge.

Stasiulis, Daiva. K. 1990. "Theorizing Connections: Gender, Race, Ethnicity and Class." In P.S. Li (ed.), *Race and Ethnic Relations in Canada*. Toronto: Oxford University Press, pp. 269–305.

Stinemetz, Jill. 1995. "Independent Schools: A Workable Solution." Unpublished paper, Department of Sociology in Education, Ontario Institute for Studies in Education, Toronto.

Suleri, Sara. 1992. *The Rhetoric of English India*. Chicago: University of Chicago Press.

Sullivan, Ann. 1995. "Realizing Successful Integrative Anti-Racist Education." Unpublished paper, Department of Sociology in Education, Ontario Institute for Studies in Education, Toronto.

Swartz, Ellen. 1992. "Emancipatory Narratives: Rewriting the Master Script in The School Curriculum." *Journal of Negro Education* 61(3): 341–55.

Taylor, Lisa. 1995. "The Implications of Multicultural and Anti-Racist Pedagogies for Teaching English as a Second Language: A Personal Reflection." Unpublished paper, Department of Sociology in Education, Ontario Institute for Studies in Education, Toronto.

Tedla, Elleni. 1995. *Sankofa: African Thought and Education*. New York: Peter Lang.

References

Thomas, Barb. 1984. "Principles of Anti-Racist Education." *Currents* 2(2): 20–24. Toronto: Urban Alliance on Race Relations.

———. 1994. "The Politics of Being White." In C. James and A. Shadd (eds.), *Encounters*. Toronto: Between the Lines.

Tierney, William. 1993a. "Academic Freedom and the Parameters of Knowledge." *Harvard Educational Review* 63(2): 143–60.

———. 1993b. *Building Communities of Difference: Higher Education in the Twenty-First Century*. Connecticut: Bergin and Garvey.

Train, Kelly. 1995. "De-Homogenizing 'Jewish Women': Essentialism and Exclusion Within Jewish Feminist Thought." MA thesis, Department of Education, University of Toronto, Toronto.

Trinh Minh ha, T. 1989. *Woman, Native, Other*. Bloomington, IN: Indiana University Press.

———. 1991. *When the Moon Waxes Red: Representation, Gender and Cultural Politics*. New York: Routledge.

Troyna, Barry (ed.). 1987. *Racial Inequality in Education*. London: Tavistock.

———. 1993. *Racism and Education: Research Perspectives*. Toronto: OISE Press.

———. 1994. "The 'Everyday World' of Teachers? Deracialized Discourses in the Sociology of Teachers and the Teaching Profession." *British Journal of Sociology of Education* 15(3): 325–39.

——— and Carol Vincent. 1995. "Equity and Education: The Discourses of Social Justice." Paper read at the Annual Meeting of the American Educational Research Association, San Francisco, CA, April 18–22.

——— and J. Williams. 1986. *Racism, Education and the State*. London: Croom Helm.

Valli, Linda. 1994. "Learning to Teach in Cross-Cultural Settings: The Significance of Personal Relations." Paper presented at the Annual Meeting of the American Educational Researchers Association, Atlanta, GA, April 4–9.

van den Berghe, Pierre. 1985. "Race and Ethnicity: A Sociobiological Perspective." In Rita M. Bienvenue and Jay Goldstein (eds.), *Ethnicity and Ethnic Relations in Canada*. Toronto: Butterworth, pp. 20–30.

wa Thiong'o, N. 1986. *Decolonising the Mind: The Politics of Language in African Literature*. London: James Currey.

Walcott, Rinaldo. 1990. "Theorizing Anti-Racist Education." *Western Canadian Anthropologist* 7(2): 109–20.

———. 1994. "The Need for a Politics of Difference." *Orbit* 25(2): 13–15.

———. 1995. "Performing the Post-Modern: Black Atlantic Rap and Identity in North America." Ph.D. dissertation, Department of Education, University of Toronto, Toronto.

Washington, V. 1982. "Racial Differences in Teacher Perceptions of First and Fourth Grade Pupils on Selected Characteristics." *Journal of Negro Education* 51(1): 60–72.

Watkins, William H. 1993. "Black Curriculum Orientations: A Preliminary Inquiry." *Harvard Educational Review* 63(3): 321–38.

Weiler, Kathleen. 1988. *Women Teaching for Change: Gender, Class and Power*. Boston, MA: Bergin and Garvey.

———. 1991. "Freire and a Feminist Pedagogy of Difference. *Harvard Educational Review* 6(4): 449–74.

Wellman, D. 1977. *Portrait of White Racism*. New York: Cambridge University Press.

West, Cornel. 1987. "Race and Social Theory." In M. Davis (ed.), *The Year Left 2*. New York: Verso, pp. 73–89.
———. 1992. *Race Matters*. Boston: Beacon Press.
White, James and Jim M. Frideres. 1977. "Race Prejudice and Racism: A Distinction." *Canadian Review of Sociology and Anthropology* 14(1): 81–90.
Williams, Eric. 1964. *Capitalism and Slavery*. London: Deutsch.
Willis, Paul. 1977. *Learning to Labour. How Working-class Kids Get Working-class Jobs*. Farnborough: Saxon House.
———. 1983. "Cultural Production and Theories of Reproduction." In L. Barton and S. Walker (eds.), *Race, Class and Education*. London: Croom Helm.
Wilson, William J. 1973. *Power, Racism and Privilege*. New York: Free Press.
Wiredu, K. 1980. *Philosophy and African Culture*. Cambridge: Cambridge University Press.
Witherspoon, R. 1987. "The Problems of Black Education." *Journal of Educational Thought* 21(23): 155–61.
Working Group. 1992. "Towards a New Beginning: The Report and Action Plan of the Four Level Government." Toronto: African-Canadian Working Group.
Wright, Handel Kashope. 1994. "Multiculturalism, Anti-Racism, Afrocentrism: The Politics of Race in Educational Praxis." *International Journal of Comparative Race and Ethnic Studies* 1(2): 13–31.
Wright, Ouida M. and Nora Allingham. 1994. "The Policy and Practice of Anti-Racist Education." *Orbit* 25(2): 4–6.
Yarmol-Franko, K. 1992. "Editorial Introduction." *Convergence* 25(1): 3–4.
Yau, M., Maisy Cheng and Suzanne Ziegler. 1993. *The 1991 Every Secondary Student Survey, Fall, Part III: Program Level and Student Achievement*. Toronto: Toronto Board of Education.
Zarate, Jose. 1994. "Indigenous Knowledge and Anti-Racist Education: Reaching Out to People and Cultures." *Orbit* 25(2): 35–36.
Zine, Jasmin. 1994. "Review of F. Barth's 'Ethnic Groups and Boundaries: The Social Organization of Cultural Difference.'" Unpublished paper, Department of Sociology in Education, Ontario Institute for Studies in Education, Toronto.
———. 1995. "The Pedagogical Implications of Cultural Differences in Learning." Unpublished paper, Department of Sociology in Education, Ontario Institute for Studies in Education, Toronto.
Zinn, M.B. 1991. *Race and the Reconstruction of Gender*. Memphis, TN: Center for Research on Women, Memphis State University, Research Paper Number 14.

Index

Index

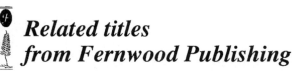

Related titles
from Fernwood Publishing

Outsider Blues: A Voice from the Shadows
Clifton Ruggles with Olivia Rovinescu

"The articles that appear in this book originate in the shadows—those marginal spaces that Black people have been forced to inhabit ever since the first slaves reached the shores of North America ..."

Ruggles tells us that "Black is more than just a racial category, it's a way of viewing the world." It is out of this set of eyes that Clifton Ruggles writes a column in the Montreal Gazette. This book is a collection of those columns and of Ruggles' photographs, which visually illustrate the "Black" experience. He tells stories of Black people everyday lives, provides non-stereotypical role models, details their contributions to culture, politics and so on—stories which are often either ignored or underplayed. Among the photographs are two photo essays, one autobiographical and one entitled *Shadowlands*. The book also includes an article by Olivia Rovinescu entitled, "Deconstructing Racism."

256 pages Photos Paper ISBN 1 895686 65 2 $19.95 Publication Date: Sept. 1996

Women in Trouble
Connecting Women's Law Violations to their Histories of Abuse
Elizabeth Comack (Manitoba)

"I never started dealing with any of this until the first time that I came to jail. I thought I was over it. But I don't think you ever really get over it."

This book addresses two areas of feminist scholarship—the recognition of violence against women and the endeavour to make visible the lives of women in prison. Beginning with women's own accounts of their troubles with the law, Elizabeth Comack uses a combination of socialist and standpoint feminism to piece together the stories of twenty-four women incarcerated for a range of offences. In the process, the women's experiences of abuse since childhood, the nature of their law violations, and the (inter)connections between the two are revealed. The book also examines whether the experience of prison enables the women to resolve their troubles and concludes by raising several questions that pertain to our efforts to respond to violence against women.

Contents: Introduction • Situating Women's Law Violations • Women's Histories of Abuse • Making Connections • The Prisoning of Women • Concluding Remarks

166 pages Paper ISBN 1 895686 61 X $14.95

Thunder in My Soul: A Mohawk Woman Speaks
Patricia Monture-Angus (Saskatchewan)

> *This is a prayer for my people and for all First Nations. It is shared with you in the spirit of gift giving. It is, in part, a reflection on my own journey down the healing road. It is also a reflection on my own struggle to shed the colonized shackles which bind my mind, my spirit and my heart.*

This book contains the reflections of one Mohawk woman and her struggles to find a good place to be in Canadian society. The essays, written in enjoyable and accessible language, document the struggles against oppression that Aboriginal people face, as well as the success and change that have come to Aboriginal communities. It is written from a woman's place. A possible text in a variety of disciplines—women's studies, Native studies, sociology, education, politics and law—it is an excellent book for anyone who wishes to better understand Aboriginal experience. It speaks to both the mind and the heart.

273 pages   Paper   ISBN 1 895686 46 $19.95

Becoming an Ally: Breaking the Cycle of Oppression
Anne Bishop (Henson/Dalhousie)

"This book is a delight to read, its language simple and clear, its examples vivid, and its message profoundly useful. It's changed the way I look at my own oppression and the way the way I do social change work. I recommend it highly."—*Diana Ralph, Social Work, Carleton University*

"The result is a book that never flinches from the hard truths of our behaviours, socially and individually, yet provides a paradigm for change."
—*Patricia Whitney, Herizons*

This book is a dialogue—by a white, lesbian feminist who co-leads with a Black colleague a workshop on racism—about the answers to questions on the nature of oppression: where does it come from, has it always been with us, what can we do to change it, what does individual healing have to do with struggles for social justice, why do members of the same oppressed group fight each other, why do some who experience oppression develop a life long commitment to fighting oppression, while others turn around and become oppressors themselves?

137 pages   Paper   ISBN 1 895686 39 3 $14.95